How to Find Your Church

How to Find Your Church

George Barna

World Wide Publications
A ministry of the Billy Graham Evangelistic Association
1303 Hennepin Avenue • Minneapolis, MN 55403

How to Find *Your* Church

© 1989 by George Barna

World Wide Publications is the publishing ministry of the Billy
Graham Evangelistic Association.

Unless otherwise noted, Scripture quotations are taken from The
Holy Bible, New International Version. Copyright © 1973, 1978,
1984 International Bible Society. Used by permission of Zondervan
Bible Publishers.

The Scripture quotation marked NKJV is taken by permission from
The New King James Version, © 1979, 1980, 1982, Thomas Nelson,
Inc., Thomas Nelson Publishers.

Library of Congress Catalog Card Number: 89-050479

ISBN: 0-89066-161-8

Printed in the United States of America

Contents

Acknowledgments   7

Preface   11

1. A Sunday-Morning Phenomenon   15
2. A Clear Sense of Purpose   23
3. Your Church-Selection Strategy   37
4. Figuring Out What a Church Believes   47
5. So Many Denominations   61
6. How Do They Worship?   75
7. Forming New Relationships   83
8. Opportunities for Involvement   93
9. Direction and Leadership   103
10. Which Is Better—Large or Small?   113
11. Church Location and Facilities   121
12. Special Programs   129
13. Making *Your* Choice   137

Appendix: Church-Visitation Review   143

Bibliography   151

Acknowledgments

No book is written without the support and encouragement of other people, whether those qualities are offered consciously or otherwise. I am deeply indebted to the friends and colleagues who have made this book possible.

Steve Griffith, of World Wide Publications, initially approached me about writing this book. Without his creative thinking, and his encouragement to take on the project, this book would not have come into existence. Besides being a wise marketer, Steve has been a good friend; my thanks to Steve for his role in this effort.

Joyce and John Saucier were among the handful of people whose reactions I sought to the initial manuscript. Their insights were stimulating and helpful. The book in its current form is a better document, thanks to their guidance.

The friends in my Bible study deserve much credit for praying me through the experience of composing this book. Suzanne and Greg Edmonson, John and Sara Graham, Tom and Cindy Sirmons, Dave and Jeannine

Crowley lent their full support to the effort, and were a source of strength for me. Sara, herself an accomplished and highly regarded writer, offered useful ideas about the manuscript.

My employees at the Barna Research Group also played a significant part in this book. Cindy Fiori assisted with the background research; Ron Sellers helped with some of the primary research; Patti Weber retyped portions of the manuscript; Jim Stipe assisted with the data tabulation process; and Julie Baum was responsible for collection of the qualitative information. Further, the development and completion of this book was a frequent topic at our company prayer meetings. Their support and encouragement was greatly appreciated.

Don Seltzer, pastor of North Coast Presbyterian Church in Encinitas, California, also deserves my thanks for consistently prodding me to continue writing. He has been one of the positive influences in my life, and has built a shining example of how a church that is excited about people can really make a difference in their lives. It is my hope that anyone in the San Diego area who reads this book and is seeking a church will visit NCPC.

Bill Deckard, my editor at World Wide Publications, provided many useful ideas that have improved the manuscript. This book is a better tool thanks to Bill's experienced editing and Christian commitment.

Before the first word was written for this book, our company conducted numerous interviews with pastors and lay people throughout the country. As always, I am grateful to those people who were willing to share their time and their lives with us. Much of what you will read is the outcome of the experiences of people located throughout America, over the course of many years. On their behalf, I hope I have captured the cumulative effect of their experiences so that you can reap the benefits of what they have already been through.

I have saved the best for last: My wife, Nancy. She supported me through verbal encouragement, prayer, sharing ideas, reviewing manuscript drafts, and restructuring her own life so that this book could come about. Nancy has earned a share of any credit that is due from this book, for the journey I allude to in the pages that follow is one which we have endured, shared, and rejoiced over together. If every marriage were blessed with someone as loving and giving as Nancy, divorce would be a concept rather than a common reality in America.

Despite the assistance of so many people, please realize that any errors, omissions, or other shortcomings must be attributed to me, not my support team.

Preface

Before you read this book, you should know a few things about me.

I believe in God. I believe that he sent Jesus Christ to earth as a bridge between sinful people and himself. Jesus was God's means for mankind to be reconciled to him, through our acceptance of salvation through faith in Christ as a gift. I have accepted Jesus Christ as my personal Savior, and know that it is something which God desires for you to do, if you have not done so already.

I also believe that God has called both you and me to become part of his family on earth—the church. It is because of this particular conviction that I have written this book.

Drive down the main streets of your community and you will encounter a number of different churches. The real question is: How can you determine which one of those churches is the best for what you need at this point in your life? This book is meant to help you think through and answer that question.

There are three sources of insight that I have drawn from in seeking answers for you. First, there has been my own experience. Over the past ten years I have visited many dozens of churches, as a visitor, a member, and a guest speaker. The vast array of impressions and insights gained from that breadth of exposure is hopefully captured in these pages. Second, we conducted extensive national research among both lay people and clergy to better understand what other people's experiences, expectations, and desires have been with regard to their selection of a church. Rather than re-invent the wheel, wouldn't it be helpful for you to know what other people found to be true as they "shopped" for a church? Wouldn't it be better to build upon *their* experience, rather than to invest your own limited resources (time, energy, patience, money) in retracing their footsteps?

Finally, I have studied the Bible to seek God's perspective on the selection of and bonding to a church. While I cannot speak for God—he does a pretty good job for himself!—I have included his admonitions as often as possible.

This book represents one perspective on selecting a church. With more than three hundred thousand local Protestant church congregations in America, the choices can be pretty bewildering. It can be like trying to select a doctor. Having no medical training, it is hard to know what to look for, or what questions to ask in order to have the right information for making your choice. Hopefully, this book will make your decision about a church more manageable.

In the end, your selection of a church is simply an expression of your commitment to God. Although this book describes elements of a selection process, and encourages you to choose a church that will offer a balance between personal support and outreach to others, it is important that you find a church and be committed to it. Writing in the New Testament, James describes a person of faith as one who is firm in commitment, not like the waves of the sea that pitch to and fro. Your commitment to a local church must be firm like that. Visit a variety of churches, examine them closely, make an informed selection—and then make that church a vital part of your life.

Just like choosing a job, a marriage partner, or a community to live in, you have many options and must weigh many factors. Pray for God's guidance. Gather as much relevant information as feasible. Make a reasoned, well-thought-through decision. And pour yourself into the worship and service of God, through the activities of your church. It will be a tremendous blessing to you.

1
A Sunday-Morning Phenomenon

You've probably shopped for a car. Maybe you've gone shopping for a house. But have you ever gone "church shopping?"

Every year, several million Americans do just that. Every Sunday morning people wake up, get dressed, have breakfast, and leave the house on a shopping excursion. No coupons to redeem, no sizes to remember, no credit cards required. These people are searching for the right church.

Some people never experience the intrigue—and the frustration—of seeking a church they can call their own. Either they were born into a church and stay with it over the years, or they have turned their backs on church altogether.

And then there are the rest of us. Of the 175 million adults currently living in America, my research shows that nearly 90 million have experienced church shopping. (I use the "shopping" terminology only because it is so descriptive; there is no intention to trivialize what is an activity of eternal importance.) There are a multitude of possible reasons behind the experience. Some people move and have to find a new congregation. Some people grow tired of the same thing, week after week, year after year, and desire a change of spiritual scenery. Other adults experience a transformation of their own spiritual awareness and maturity, and recognize that their current church is stifling, rather than encouraging, their personal spiritual growth.

And every year, there are literally millions of Americans who, despite religious training as youths, have fallen away from organized religion during their early adult years, but suddenly notice the resulting void in their lives. As one step toward greater wholeness and fulfillment, they decide that church may have something to offer them after all. At the very least, they feel it is worth giving the church another chance.

One Man's Journey

If any of these descriptions portray your own situation, realize that you are not alone in your quest for a church home. In fact, I have been through the church-shopping maze several times, and have been both fascinated and frustrated by the experience.

My initial foray into church exploration came after I was married. My wife and I decided that as a newly married couple, we needed to grow together in as many ways as possible—a thorough bonding of mind, body, and spirit. So we set out to find a church with which we both felt comfortable and satisfied.

Very quickly we discovered how little we knew about organized religion in America. We had no idea how to even identify the church options available to us. After some rather clumsy attempts at enumerating the possibilities, we realized we weren't quite sure what we were looking for. In frustration—and naivete—we agreed that we would "know it when we found it."

Then we began visiting churches. In retrospect, what a funny pattern we followed. Without any idea of what these churches stood for, how they differed, or what to expect, we went to Catholic, Presbyterian, Baptist, and non-denominational churches. We finally settled on one church; but still we felt bewildered from all the experiences and impressions of our search.

Several years later, we moved cross-country. Once again we were confronted with the need to find a church. By this time we had a stronger sense of our own spiritual needs and gifts. This time, we entered the marketplace with a shopping list of factors to evaluate.

Unfortunately, we were also trying to replicate the happiness we had found at our previous church. As a result, we kept looking for a carbon copy of that church. Six months and thirteen churches later, we realized that we could not reasonably expect to relive our past. We were trying to fit each church into a very narrow set of specifications: but a church is like a human being—it is a living entity, and just like you and me, it cannot easily be pigeon-holed and categorized, and it certainly cannot satisfy every whim on a wish list of attributes.

With some discouragement, my wife and I "settled" for a church that felt right, even though it was absolutely nothing like our previous church. Different denomination. Different style of worship. Thirty times larger (literally—we went from a church with a hundred members to one with three thousand!). Some of the new church's beliefs were different, although the primacy of Jesus Christ as Savior, and the centrality of the Bible, were consistent. Our old church and our new one were about as similar as night and day. Yet, somehow, the choice seemed right for us, at that time in our lives.

Three years later, we moved again. Interestingly, the only thing we dreaded about the move was having to leave our church and find a new one. Yet we were relocating to a part of the midwest which was known for its spiritual fervor, and we were confident that there was a great church just waiting for us.

Well, there was. Unfortunately, it took us another six months and fourteen churches to find it. But this time, the moment we set foot in the church, we knew it was meant for us. During our years in that area, the church became the focal point of our lives. In fact, that church totally changed our lives.

So you can imagine what a heartbreak it was to move once again, two years later. But this time, we figured it would be easy. We were simply returning to the same city that we had moved away from two and a half years earlier. We were certain that this time we could simply renew our membership and friendships at our old church, and get back in the swing of things.

Another lesson learned. You cannot live in the past. Even though we returned to the same church— same worship service, same pastors, same Sunday-school classes—it was very different. Many of our old friends had moved away. Others had left for new churches. And we found that during our time in the midwest, involved in another church, we ourselves had changed in some important, fundamental ways.

Thus we began what was to be our fourth church-shopping experience. Eventually we found a church that met many of our needs, and where we hoped we could use our talents to help serve the congregation.

After two years of committed attendance, financial support, and other involvement, we decided it was not the right church for us, after all. Why had it taken two years to come to that conclusion? For a long time, we struggled with guilt. We had convinced ourselves that since it was a growing, Bible-believing, Bible-teaching church, with several thousand happy members, we must be wrong to feel unfulfilled and dissatisfied. Yes, the teaching was unparalleled. And the people were so dedicated to serving Christ and supporting that church. What was our problem?

I eventually reached a breaking point. To attend the services, Sunday after Sunday, was simply a game. I had already emotionally divorced myself from that body, and my physical presence was now an empty demonstration of Christian obedience. In my heart I desperately wanted a family of Christian people with whom I could worship, communicate, volunteer my energies, and study the Word of God. If the church I was attending did not facilitate that experience, then it was my responsibility to rectify the situation.

There was nothing wrong with that church. There was nothing wrong with me, either. No need for guilt or assigning blame. It's like a man and a woman who are dating each other. Perhaps they date for two or three years. They get to know each other. At some point, they know each other well enough to realize that they are not meant for each other. That doesn't mean that they are failures, or that they should give up dating for as long as they live. They simply were not called by God to spend their lives together. That should be a wonderful, freeing insight, one that leads to continued exploration and growth.

And so began my fifth—and to date, final—search for a church home. This time, with a much keener sense of what I was looking for, the search was short and concise.

The church my wife and I currently attend is far

from perfect. It does not satisfy every item on my wish list. But it is a church that enables me to satisfy the needs that I, as a Christian seeking to worship and serve God, have identified as most critical.

So, I have shopped for a church when I didn't have one to start with, when I moved to a new community, and when I felt that the church I had joined was no longer the right one for me. In the process, I've learned a lot—about God, about the church as an institution, about other people, and about myself.

Perhaps you have been in one or all of these situations. Or perhaps your interest in finding a church springs from an entirely different set of circumstances. The key is that you have taken the first step to solving the puzzle; that is, you have decided that exploring the various churches in your area is a worthwhile investment of your time.

My purpose in writing this book is to share with you some of my experiences and insights related to church evaluation and selection. There is no magic, proven formula to guide everyone through this process. But I do believe there are some basic principles you can use to help make the process more efficient and fulfilling.

In preparation for this book, my research company interviewed a nationwide sample of several hundred people concerning their experiences in looking for the right church. The research was quite revealing. It detailed the perspectives and experiences of people who searched for a church and never did find one they could adopt. It revealed many others who had found a satisfying church. It gave the viewpoint of people who have been born into a church and have never felt the urge to leave or to look elsewhere. And the research provided reactions from priests and ministers, the religious professionals whose job it is to offer worthy spiritual homes.

This book, then, is the result of the trials, the tribulations, and the wisdom of many who share your interest in being part of a church. The objective of this book is to help you prepare for the church-evaluation and selection process by identifying and reflecting upon some of the factors that others have found to be important.

I believe that being an active member of a church is part of God's desire for our lives. In reading the Bible over the years, I have come to understand that the church is God's family (i.e., his people, brought together by their mutual love for him) and that it must become our family, too. The church has much to offer to each of us, and we, in return, have special talents that can help to make our church a vibrant, joyful, and successful family of believers.

Be encouraged! Yes, finding the right church might take some time, with fits of frustration emerging en route. But my experience—and the experience of millions of Americans who have gone through the church-evaluation and selection process—is that the outcome more than justifies the difficult journey.

2
A Clear Sense
of Purpose

Some years ago, I worked for an advertising agency. One day, a week or so before Christmas, the president of the agency called on his secretary to perform an important company mission.

"I think we have a great shot at winning the XYZ account," he began. "Let's get their CEO a Christmas present. I want you to go out today and get that gift. Make sure it's something appropriate, and something different. I want him to know that we are creative, so don't just get a box of candy for him. And keep the cost reasonable."

That was all the direction she was able to get out of our boss. She spent hours that day and the next, going from store to store, hunting for the perfect, albeit unknown gift. Why was it so difficult? She knew absolutely nothing about the CEO whose gift she was seeking. She had no clues about his taste, his interests, or his needs. She had no clear concept of how much money her boss would consider "reasonable," nor what would seem both appropriate and different to the recipient of the gift.

Unfortunately, many people search for a church with the same handicaps. Prior to embarking upon their "church search," they fail to clarify in their own minds why they feel the urge to be part of a church. Perhaps they have not clearly identified the qualities and characteristics that they feel are most important for their "ideal church" to possess. Often, people restrict their search to churches with which they are already familiar, thus limiting the universe of possibilities, and possibly overlooking churches that may be exactly what they are seeking. Others have not truly prepared for a successful search. Simply deciding that it would be nice to have a meaningful church experience on a regular basis is not enough. To satisfy that desire requires a commitment to the process of finding the right church.

As you read the pages that follow, keep in mind that the purpose of this book is to help you discover your own ideas and needs related to church involvement, to evaluate the congregations you are considering, and to make the choice that will maximize your spiritual development.

What Is a Church?

For the sake of clarity, let's agree upon what a church is.

The ideal source of a definition of the church is the Bible. Why? Because it is through God's words to us, as imparted through the Bible, that we can understand why he created the concept and the reality of the church. Church was God's idea, not man's. If we wish to derive the greatest possible benefit from our church experience, we ought to study what the originator of the idea had in mind.

God wants the church to reveal his own glory to the entire world:

> His intent was that now, through the church, the manifold wisdom of God should be made known to the rulers and authorities in the heavenly realms. (Ephesians 3:10; see also, John 17).

Through the activities of the people who comprise Christian churches, others can observe and experience the very character of God. The manner in which Christians worship him, the values they live by, and the different perspective they have on the meaning of life differentiate them from all other faiths and peoples. A true Christian church is one which has God at its center; all activities and thoughts are based upon the church's goal of worshiping God and sharing him in tangible ways with the world.

The church is a group of people—not a building, or a place, or a denomination. There are churches that meet in people's living rooms, and there are churches that do not have a denominational affiliation or even a name. By God's definition, a church is a group of people that he has called together to praise him and to serve him:

> ... that we, who were the first to hope in Christ, might be for the praise of his glory. (Ephesians 1:12; see also, John 4:23-24; Romans 15:7-12)

The term "community of believers" is synonymous with the word "church" and may be more descriptive. It conveys a group of people who have a common faith in God, and who are united by their love for him to do things which will show the world their love of God.

The church is also a place where people can be edified—that is, a place that provides guidance for all that we do. The Bible is the guidebook, and the church is the place where the people who are reading that book share their insights with each other. The church is the place where ultimate truth from the Bible is revealed, and the practical application of that truth to our daily struggles and dreams can take shape. Through prayer, discussion, and other experiences, the body brought together as the local church can grow as human beings seeking to know and serve God.

While we read in the Bible that the main purpose of mankind is to know God and serve him, we also read that this is to be a joyful, fulfilling responsibility:

> You have made known to me the path of life; you will fill me with joy in your presence, with eternal pleasures at your right hand. (Psalm 16:11; see also, John 16:24; 17:13)

And it is through our church involvement that we can better experience the fullness of a meaningful relationship with the living God. It is the love and understanding of our spiritual brothers and sisters that helps us make it through the trials we encounter. It is through the mutual struggle for insight into God's ways for our lives that we can gain and maintain a heavenly perspective on our mission on earth. And it is through commitment to our spiritual family—the church—that we can share the joy of having an exciting and growing relationship with God.

When you ponder the type of church you are seeking, do not think of it as merely a place where sermons are preached and music is sung every Sunday morning. That is an incomplete understanding of a Christian church, as God called it into being. Jesus called the church his "bride"—a living being with which he has an intimate and growing relationship that knows no bounds. (Ephesians 5:25-27, 29-32; Revelation 21:2-4;)

Your Reasons for Belonging

Before you get started on your church search, it is valuable to "lay all of your cards on the table." Identify exactly *why* you want to be involved with a church, and what are your expectations of the church. If you do not know why you are pursuing a church, or what specific characteristics and qualities you are looking for, the chances are greatly enhanced that you will not find your "ideal" church. We are embarking on a journey that will culminate in a decision that has major, dramatic consequences for your life. It is worth devoting time up front to clarify your own motives and expectations.

As you think about why you want to be part of a church, be totally honest with yourself. You don't necessarily have to share your selection criteria with other people, if you find that to be embarrassing or personal. But if you are to have a chance of making the best choice, you must have a complete knowledge of your motivations.

If some of your motivations seem selfish, admit it: denial of those interests will only make your search more frustrating. For instance, some people seek a new church in order to meet new friends, or to have a place where their children can be taught good values. Other people we interviewed described personal problems they were experiencing, and stated that their search was stimulated by the hope that a church would have some answers and thereby reduce the tensions in their life. These reasons may not sound as spiritual as "I want to worship God" or "I need to praise Jesus for the way he has blessed me," but they are no less valid and important.

If some of your motivations for seeking a church seem unexciting or unsophisticated, that's okay too. Maybe you don't know much about God, Jesus Christ, or religion, and simply want to explore the Christian faith. Perhaps you attended church as a child, stopped going when you were older, and now feel an urge to give church another try. God is not seeking a relationship with you or me because we can outwit him or outperform him. He knows what we think and what is in our hearts even better than we do. Our objective is simply to learn about God in a more personal and substantial way, by joining the spiritual family he has prepared for us at a local church.

Many others have sweated through the church-selection process before you, and emerged more confident about their faith and their church as a result of their struggle to make the best choice. Let me describe some of the reasons they gave for their church shopping. (These are people who went on to find great fulfillment from church involvement.) Not surprisingly, we found that many of those reasons are totally consistent with what the Bible says a church will do in a person's life.

You may find that your own list of reasons for seeking a church has many parallels with the attributes I'm about to mention. Or, you may find that your list is very different. Realize that we are not trying to differentiate "right" reasons from "wrong" ones. The goal is simply to determine why you need a church, so that you can find the church that best fits your own needs. Perhaps after reading through the reasons listed below, you'll want to add a few of them to your list.

A. Relationship With God

The majority of people who are "happily churched" say that their involvement with a local congregation was born out of a desire to better know God. The Bible speaks of our need to pursue a person-to-person relationship with God:

> My soul yearns, even faints for the courts of the Lord; my heart and my flesh cry out for the living God. (Psalm 84:2; see also, 73:25; Isaiah 26:9; Acts 17:22-28)

And it shows us that God created the church as one means of nurturing that relationship. (Ephesians 4:11-16) It is through the church—that special group of people who believe in him and desire to worship and serve him—that we are able to learn about God. Through the church we experience God's presence and peace, his love and acceptance; and we serve him with the skills and talents he has given us.

Why should we concern ourselves about having a relationship with God? Because he created us specifically for that purpose! When mankind disrupted that relationship by sinning against him, he took the initiative and created a way of continuing and strengthening the bond—through the death and resurrection of his Son, Jesus Christ.

God designated the church as one channel through which those who have chosen to believe in him can grow closer to him. This happens through sincere prayer, preaching, and teaching based upon the Bible, music offered as a gift to glorify him, the confession of our sins against him, and the encouragement from the church to maintain and heighten our commitment to him.

B. *Relationships With Other People*

Part of God's plan is for each of us to live in relationship with other people. He created us as social beings, with the ability to communicate with each other, to enjoy and support each other.

The church was designated to be a place where people of like minds and like hearts could come together and share their common love for God. It is a place where people can realize a special kinship with each other because of that spiritual commonality. A church that follows the biblical pattern is one in which people are loved, not judged; where they are accepted for who they are, not for what society holds to be dear.

The interviews conducted for this book indicated that the people who are most satisfied with their church also found that most of their friends came from that church. Thus, a sound church is one where people who are serious about God can meet others of like interests, and develop meaningful and lasting relationships with each other.

C. *Real Answers to Tough Questions*

Often, people decide to look for a church during or after a period of major trauma. It could be the death of a loved one, the loss of a job, the dissolution of a significant relationship, a debilitating injury, or any of hundreds of other possibilities. The traumatic event is the catalyst to raising difficult questions. In the quest for answers, many people turn to religion, through the church.

In other cases, it is not a traumatic event, but a nagging uncertainty that elevates one's consideration of the church as a place to seek answers. Many "baby boomers," for instance, are struggling with the reason for living, and searching for real happiness. After years of devotion to "getting ahead" by the world's standards, they have made it—big house, expensive cars, exotic vacations, prestigious corporate titles, healthy children. Yet, having all of that has left them a bit empty; they're king of the hill, but the hill seems inconsequential now that they're on top of it. What they believed would bring happiness, joy, and contentment, instead brought disillusionment and a yearning of the heart. Many have turned to the church, in the hope that through an understanding of God and their own spiritual needs, they can come to grips with the meaning of life, and why things that appeared so alluring and meaningful turned out to be so one-dimensional and vacuous.

This process of experiencing frustrations and turning to the church—often as an option of last resort—has been going on for centuries. Interestingly, although many other man-made institutions have come and gone over the course of those centuries, the Christian church continues to exist and thrive, because the church *does* have real answers to life's toughest questions and most difficult situations.

Those answers come in the form of a true confrontation and personal relationship with God. They come in the form of insight through biblical principles, either taught through the spoken word or gleaned from the reading of Scripture. They come in the comfort, support, and reassurance provided by other church members—some of whom empathize, others of whom sympathize, but all of whom express God's love through their concern and interest.

In many cases, the church is the *only* institution that has real answers to the major challenges we face.

D. Helping Others

One of the most endearing qualities of the average American adult is the desire to make a positive difference in the lives of other people. That's right, the same people who honk at you on the highway, who give you a hard time in the shopping mall, or who irritate you with their self-indulgence, also have a desire to do good things for the benefit of other people.

The church is one outlet through which people can join together to have a discernible, positive impact on the lives of others. Every person on the face of the earth has special needs that require attention—financial, psychological, social, emotional, spiritual, or combinations thereof. A central purpose of the church is to enable each individual to recognize the special talents, skills, and spiritual gifts he or she has, and to provide a forum for the practical use of those abilities.

People feel better about themselves when they are able to help others. It is healthy to focus on something other than ourselves; it is good to feel that the world is a better place because we have something to contribute. When a church facilitates such activity it breathes new life into those who are helped, and those who are helping.

E. Transmitting Values

Much has been written about the baby-boom generation, the seventy-six million Americans born from 1946 to 1964. They are the young adults of America. Recent research among the boomers indicates that many of them are now returning to church after an extended absence.

Why? Because now *they* have school-aged children of their own, and believe that the behaviors, attitudes, and values taught by the Christian church should be a part of their children's upbringing. Many of these parents are bringing their children to church to insure that their youngsters learn about matters such as love, acceptance, God, forgiveness, and charity.

But beyond parenting needs, there is also a broad segment of the adult population that perceives the church to be the "moral gatekeeper" of America. The church is looked upon to provide a measure of moral and ethical stability and consistency in a world which is characterized by constantly changing rules of conduct. The church is a source of absolutes in a world of relatives, a pillar of eternal truths amid a sea of uncertainty and deception. Belonging to a church facilitates moral sensitivity, while at the same time it offers implicit support for a Christian moral and ethical code.

F. Outlet for Talents

God has provided every human being with special skills and talents that help to set us apart from other people. One of the most exciting aspects of being involved in a church is having the opportunity to use those skills and talents for the benefit of other people, the benefit of the church at large, and for our own personal fulfillment.

Churches are, by nature, volunteer organizations. Most are managed by full-time, paid ministers and perhaps some staff associates. However, there is a tremendous need for the people of the congregation to pitch in and do the work of the church. This might entail efforts such as singing, teaching, typing, writing, cooking, or many other activities. The church is dependent upon its members using their skills to enable the work of the church to get done.

G. *Convenience*

Our research revealed that many people initially chose a church because it was located close to their home, or because it was easy to get to. Usually, this was not the sole factor upon which the church was selected, but was an important consideration.

Studies conducted by church growth specialists have found that most people pick a church that is located within five miles of their home. Why? Given the busy schedules of most Americans, the last thing they want is to have to drive a long distance on Sunday mornings to get to their church. Many people also stated that it was more difficult to build close and meaningful relationships with people who did not live close to them. Other people explained that they wanted a church close to their home so that they could feel that it was truly a church serving the needs and people of their own neighborhood. In that way, they felt that whatever resources they gave to the church would benefit the people in their immediate area.

H. *Denomination*

"I grew up in that denomination" was a common explanation as to why people chose their current church. Having spent years growing familiar with the doctrines, the traditions, and the practices of a specific denomination, many people naturally revert to a church within that same denomination, even if they have since turned their back on the denomination for a period of years.

I. Beliefs and Practices

A critical factor for many newcomers is what the church believes, and how it lives those beliefs. Certainly, one of the key purposes of a church is to provide spiritual teaching to people. And that teaching is of little value if it remains mere "head knowledge." Religion is only useful when it becomes a lifestyle, a series of principles and a set of values that transforms the way in which we live to conform to what God desires.

Often, church shoppers evaluate a church based upon how the people in the congregation act—not on Sunday morning, but when they are not on the church grounds. How members of the church react under the pressure of the job, the family, or the marketplace may be a better indication of whether or not the church is really providing something that makes a difference in the lives of its members.

J. Obedience

The Bible teaches that being an active member of a God-centered church, one that preaches salvation by grace through faith, one that bases its teaching on the Bible, is an obligation to which God will hold Christians accountable. Why? Because the church is the family he has prepared for us, the place where we can come to get our priorities right, an institution which enables us to recharge our spiritual batteries when they run low. To put it another way, the failure to be an active member of a church is an act of disobedience against God.

Does this mean that it is wrong to spend time searching for a church, leaving behind some of these sincere, godly groups of people as not relevant for our own lives? No. Your period of examination and exploration is a valuable time of getting to know more about the totality of God's family. Some churches may not be a good fit for you, just as you do not necessarily marry the first person you date. By observing and participating in other church traditions and experiences, you are forced to clarify who you are, what you want out of your relationship with God, what you are willing to put into a relationship with God, and the nature and function of a church that will enable you to realize your full potential spiritual maturity. The church-shopping experience may well enable you to transform your perspective of Christianity from being an amorphous, worldwide, impersonal activity to one that is highly personalized, interconnected, and important to you.

The Next Step

Now that you have determined why you wish to be part of a church, it will be easier to prioritize the factors that will play a part in your decision. And that is what the next chapter is all about.

3
Your Church-Selection Strategy

A friend of mine had been driving his car for more than a decade. Not exactly a mechanical wizard, he had put off trading in his dilapidated, unreliable vehicle for longer than even he cared to admit. Finally, the inevitable happened: En route to work one morning his car died, never to start again. At last, he was face-to-face with the necessity of having to purchase another car.

The day after the mechanical death of his auto, he visited the lots of a handful of car dealers. After a full day of looking at new and used cars, and listening to the pitches of the salesmen, he returned home more confused than when he had begun. He felt particularly pressured because he needed his car to get to and from work—relying on friends to transport him was a solution which neither he nor his friends considered to be long-term or acceptable.

After a sleepless night, he made his choice, and bought a car the following day. Unfortunately, since he really had never stopped to clarify in his own mind just what he was looking for, he was not convinced that his decision was the best one he could have made. Sure enough, for the years that he owned that car, he was never really satisfied, always harboring doubts about his choice, and pondering what kind of automobile he could have acquired if he had taken the proper steps to making an informed choice.

An *informed choice.* Whenever you make a major decision—whom to marry, which house to buy, what job offer to accept, which church to attend—you need as much relevant information as possible upon which to make your decision. You also need a plan or a strategy to enable you to use information effectively toward making the best choice.

Let's briefly consider one strategy for helping you determine what you will base your selection of a church upon.

The Game Plan

Your goal is to choose the best church—the one which will prove to be most satisfying and will address your needs most effectively.

The challenge is to develop criteria which you can use to evaluate the available options (i.e., churches). Determining the most important criteria is not, in itself, enough: you must also prioritize those criteria. Ultimately, what you need is a means of separating which church-selection factors mean a lot to you from those that mean relatively little.

The list below contains some examples of the criteria you may wish to use in evaluating the churches you visit. These are the criteria suggested by the people interviewed in the survey conducted for this book—based upon their own church-shopping experiences.

You will probably notice that there is a strong correlation between the reasons they described (above) for seeking a church, and those qualities which they identified as selection criteria. Naturally, once you have determined why you want to be connected with a church, and what the key characteristics and qualities of the church may be, those can be translated into specific qualities you look for in the churches you visit.

Some evaluation criteria:

A. The spiritual beliefs of the church
B. The lifestyles of the church members
C. The denomination with which the church is affiliated
D. The ability to make meaningful relationships with people in the church
E. The potential for using your skills and talents to serve others, or to experience personal fulfillment
F. The ability to have a significant worship experience
G. The size of the congregation
H. The depth of vision and quality of leadership evident within the church
I. The special programs the church operates (e.g., Sunday school, small group Bible studies, missions projects, etc.)
J. The location of the church and its members in relation to your home
K. The facilities and equipment owned by the church

The list could continue, with every individual

identifying additional aspects that are directly relevant to his or her needs and interests. The point, however, is that unlike my friend who searched for a car without knowing what he was looking for and without a plan for evaluating the cars he was shown, you can be a smart "consumer" in your quest for a church.

By now, you have at least determined why you want to become active in a church. That's a huge first step. With those reasons in mind, it will be much easier for you to identify the decision-making criteria you will use, and to assign a relative value to each of those criteria.

In the appendix of this book is a form which might help you in this process. It is only a model, a sample which you should modify to meet your own needs. The idea is for you to determine how important the different factors are to you in the church selection you will make. By doing so, you will be more aware of these factors when you visit churches, and thus gain a more realistic perspective of what the church has to offer.

Using the form to determine how well each church rates, in light of your expectations, will help you to better recall what you experienced. (After all, it's hard to remember what the first church you visited was like after you visit ten or twelve!) It will also assist you in arriving at a more reasoned, logical assessment of what each church is like.

Each of the remaining chapters of this book provide you with a fuller perspective on the criteria listed above. Only you, however, can determine just how important each of those factors is for you. Don't be surprised if you have one or two criteria that are absent from the list presented here. Just add yours to the list, and drop those which do not apply.

The Rest of the Process

After you have developed a set of criteria for evaluating the churches you will visit, you need to create a list of all the churches you are willing to visit. It is probably best to develop as comprehensive a list as possible at the outset, and then pare it back, based upon the criteria you have developed.

Where can you find out what churches are available? The most reliable sources are the Yellow Pages of the telephone book, your friends, and your local chamber of commerce. Some people start by listing churches they know of that are within a reasonable distance from their home, then adding others to the list as they are identified.

Once you have developed a comprehensive list, you can start reducing the possibilities, even before you visit your first church, by comparing the known characteristics of the churches with the specifics which you are looking for. For instance, there are usually some churches that can be dropped from consideration immediately because of their distance from your home, or perhaps because of the denominational affiliation of the church. If those are critical criteria for you, and several churches do not meet your requirements, you can save yourself some time and aggravation by scratching them from the list in the early going.

Once you have narrowed the list of possibilities, develop a visitation schedule. The order in which you visit the churches is important. Interestingly, many people find that while their church-shopping adventure is time consuming, they learn a lot from the experience, and are often surprised by much of what they see or hear. Thus, it might be advantageous to randomly order the churches on your schedule, and gain the benefit of the broadest possible exposure to new ideas and practices.

After each visit to a church, you should make some notes, or fill in an evaluation sheet (like the one in the appendix). In some cases, you may wish to visit a church several times, to get a better feel for what that church is like. This is especially true if you happen to visit a church during a weekend when the pastor is not present, and a substitute speaker is filling in. (You can avoid this situation by calling the church ahead of time and asking if the pastor will be preaching; this is especially important during the summer months, when pastors take their vacations or study leaves.)

At some point, you may find the church that is just what you are looking for, and wish to discontinue your search. That's great! There is no virtue in church shopping for the sake of church shopping. The goal, of course, is for you to find the right church, not to conduct an exhaustive search so that you become an expert on your local churches. If you know beyond a doubt that you have found the right church, say a prayer of thanks and start becoming a part of that church family!

Many people never experience that certainty, though. You may visit all of the churches on your list before you make the final determination. There is nothing wrong with such thoroughness, and I would expect you to be every bit as elated about your ultimate selection as the person who interrupted the church-shopping process after finding what he or she was looking for.

A common approach is to not only visit all of the churches on your list, but then to narrow down your selection to a handful of churches that you re-visit. You may go back to those "finalists" once, twice, or any number of times before making your selection. You might visit some of the finalists once and others multiple times. With so many church experiences under your belt, you will undoubtedly refine your understanding of what you desire in a church; you may even wonder how one or two of the churches ever got to be among the final few. Whatever course you follow, take your best shot at making a choice, and then dive into the life of that church with enthusiasm and anticipation.

A Word of Caution

As people around the country were quick to point out in our research, you only get out of a church what you put in. The people who simply put on their nice clothing, drive to church, listen to the sermon, and drive home again generally find their church experience to be of limited value. The people who understand that a church is nothing more than the sum of all its parts—i.e., the efforts of all the members—and who devote themselves to making the church a fulfilling (and fun!) place to be, find that their church is an integral part of their lives.

In America, we have become accustomed to performances. We turn on the television, we go to the movies, we attend sports events or concerts, we play pre-recorded video cassettes, and we wait to be entertained. But God did not intend for church to be a house of entertainment.

That does not mean church should be boring—far from it: any place that is helping us to understand the God of creation, the Savior of mankind, and providing an outlet for personal relationships and the use of our talents and skills, should be as exciting a place as can be found on the face of the earth! Many churches have found that they can provide a contemporary format or expression of worship and teaching which makes the service more lively and more meaningful to some people. And, of course, churches can sponsor events, apart from the Sunday-morning experience, that are designed to provide the best in entertainment, for any of a variety of laudable purposes.

However, when you examine a church, remember that the way *not* to evaluate the church is based upon the quality or entertainment value of a religious performance—i.e., how perfectly the choir sang, or how eloquently the preacher spoke, or how meticulously the ushers were dressed. More properly, think about what impact the sermon had upon your life, or how well the singing led you to worship God, or how the friendliness of the people made you want to be warm to somebody else. The purpose of the church is to transform our lives through the development and enhancement of our relationship with God, through Jesus Christ and the Holy Spirit. The church is not called to act as a spiritual babysitter.

Throughout your church-selection effort, one of the most effective tools you can employ is prayer. Prayer is our means of communicating with God. So pray often, asking God to give you the experiences, insights, and wisdom that will enable you to make the best choice. God will grant those desires of your heart which coincide with his plan for your life—but you need to ask him for that blessing. You don't have to pray for long periods of time, or with fancy words, or even out loud. Just tell him, in your own way, what you are seeking, and ask for his help. Then move forward, firmly believing that he will grant that desire.

Finally, realize that, like in a family, there will be a

time of transition, in which you have to work through the difficulties of becoming a part of a family that was already existent. In a way, you become like an adopted child. The family that adopts you was probably getting along just fine without you, although they are very happy that you are now part of the clan. Despite the happiness, they will have to change some of their ways to accommodate your needs—and you will have to do the same, to become an accepted part of the family. A church, like an individual, cannot be all things to all people. But it can become a loving and caring unit that makes your life so much better, just as you can enhance the life of that family.

4
Figuring Out What a Church Believes

There are many organizations, other than a church, which you could join, ranging from sports and fitness centers to special-interest clubs and community-service groups. Chances are that your interest in becoming part of a church is related, to some degree, to the driving force behind its very existence: its spiritual beliefs.

For thousands of years, people have had sharp divisions of opinion about spiritual beliefs, sometimes resulting in social revolutions or wars. Expressions like "fight for what you believe in" were probably born during tense moments in history when the inhabitants of a particular community were threatened because they refused to adopt the religious beliefs and customs of an opposing army. Needless to say, if you feel you must know exactly what a church believes before you can agree to become part of that church, you are not setting a precedent!

The idea of evaluating a church on the basis of its beliefs is compelling. However, in a practical sense, how can you really do that? After all, literally thousands of books have been written about theology and spiritual doctrine, with every author providing many different perspectives and discussion points. There are many levels of beliefs that could be examined—beliefs about church structure and government, beliefs about the Trinity, beliefs about the creation of the world, beliefs about the purpose of mankind.

If you have ever been involved in an argument about religious doctrine, you may have learned—the hard way—that while there are numerous details which can be argued indefinitely, many of those ideas simply are not important enough to devote significant time to. As in every walk of life, there are certain central ideas and beliefs that form the foundation of any particular church. If you are trying to understand that church, your best bet is to focus upon those foundational concepts. Once you understand those, you will be in a better position to make a judgment.

There may be many fundamental ideas about the Christian faith with which you are not familiar. To find a church, you do not need to be a highly trained theologian. Perhaps, though, your exploration of churches and their beliefs will help you to clarify the critical issues associated with your faith.

Again relying upon the experiences and reactions of people who have been down the church-shopping route before us, here are a few areas of belief that our forebears have found to be worth the time and effort to examine.

Beliefs About God

One of the most basic characteristics of any church is its beliefs about God. Since I have assumed that we are only addressing choices among Christian churches, we can also assume that such churches believe in the existence of God. What we need to explore, then, is their beliefs *about* God.

One of the aspects of my own journey that has been most fascinating is how different the beliefs of churches can be about the very nature of God. One such area of difference concerns the "Trinity." The Bible teaches that God is a Trinity—one Being comprised of three persons united in being and purpose. These three persons are God the Father, God the Son (Jesus Christ), and God the Holy Spirit. This "triune" God has no equal, and he is the only true God in existence. Does the church you are considering teach these things about God? (Matthew 3:16-17; 28:19; John 15:26; Acts 5:3-4; 2 Corinthians 13:14; Hebrews 1:8; 1 Peter 1:2)

Another characteristic of God is that he is eternal and unchanging. This means that he has always existed: he has no beginning and no end—a concept that is consistent with the belief that he is the Creator of all things. The fact that he is eternal and unchanging is of critical importance to us as Christians: only if God is eternal can we have any real hope of eternal life. And if God was constantly waffling and changing plans, like human beings, we could never have total assurance of salvation. But he is the same yesterday, today, and tomorrow—and it is upon the basis of that consistency that we have a secure faith:

> Every good and perfect gift is from above, coming down from the Father of the heavenly lights, who does not change like shifting shadows. (James 1:17; see also, Malachi 3:6)

Does the church you are visiting teach that God is eternal and unchanging?

Churches also have different perspectives on the attributes and powers of God. A study of the Scriptures reveals that God knows everything that has, is, and will ever happen. This is known as "omniscience":

> Nothing in all creation is hidden from God's sight. Everything is uncovered and laid bare before the eyes of him to whom we must give account. (Hebrews 4:13; see also, Psalm 147:5; Proverbs 15:3; Romans 11:33; 1 John 3:20)

God also commands all power; he is able to do anything he wants, when he wants to do so. This is known as "omnipotence." (Genesis 1:1-3;18:14; Job 42:2; James 4:12-15) And God is present in all places, at all times: He is "omnipresent." (Psalm 139:7-12; Jeremiah 23:23-24) A church that fails to acknowledge that God has these attributes is one which limits his power and majesty. If you are seriously seeking to know and serve the God revealed in the Bible, be sure that your church has a proper theological perspective about God's qualities.

It sometimes helps to gain a perspective on a church's teaching about the *moral* attributes of God. Some of the key elements of God's moral personality are that he is loving, holy, righteous and just, and merciful. Yet, some churches confuse his character, and describe him as an angry God, one whose justice is vindictive rather than vindicating. (Deuteronomy 4:31; Psalm 99:9; 116:5; Ephesians 2:4; 1 John 4:8-16)

What about God's relationship with mankind? Does he seek to develop a personal relationship with us, or does he remain distant from us, uninvolved in our lives until we meet him on the Day of Judgment? Think about the implications of this for your involvement in a church. How could any warmth of fellowship be found in a church which believed that God has no interest in relating to us? Quite to the contrary, the Bible teaches that God not only wants to have a personal relationship with us, but gave up his only begotten Son to make such a relationship possible. A church which fully teaches and understands that truth will be a place where sincere love and friendship are more likely to be found.

There are other aspects about the church's view of God that you may wish to examine. There is an ongoing controversy about the issue of creation. Many people— and churches—assert that the earth was created by something other than God, and that man came about through a process of evolution. The traditional Christian position is that God existed before anything else, and chose to create all that exists. Even within the Christian community, there is debate over whether the creation account in Bible should be interpreted to mean that God created the universe in seven twenty-four-hour days, or simply seven periods of time. What are the beliefs of the churches you visit concerning God's role in creation?

Of great practical importance to each of us is what we believe to be God's role in our lives. Does God care about our every action? Does he become involved in our lives in a personal way? Can we actually know what God wants from us while we are living? What about the concept of "free will"? Has he given us the freedom (and responsibility) to respond to conditions as we see fit, or has he pre-determined everything we will do, removing the choice from our realm?

Beliefs About Jesus Christ

There are several schools of thought about Jesus Christ. The traditional Christian perspective is that he was the true Son of God, who became a man so that God could re-establish a relationship with mankind, a relationship that had been broken through our sin against him. Alternative viewpoints suggest that Jesus was simply a great teacher or religious leader who did walk the face of the earth and even performed miracles, but was not a part of the triune God.

Churches have divergent views about the death and resurrection of Jesus. Beliefs about Christ's resurrection are particularly important, for if the resurrection did not happen, there has been no victory over sin, and mankind is still out of relationship with God. Indeed, if the resurrection did not occur as explicitly outlined in the Bible, then the veracity of the Bible itself is in doubt.

Some argue about the role of Christ in people's lives today. As with God the Father, they teach that Christ is a distant deity not intimately involved with human beings. Understanding the teaching of any church on the life, death, resurrection, and present-day activity of Jesus Christ is of central importance.

The Role of the Holy Spirit

Some churches place a very strong emphasis on the existence and activity of the Holy Spirit, while others virtually ignore him. Teachings probably vary more widely on the role of the Holy Spirit than on the being and character of either God the Father or Jesus Christ (God the Son). Since most Christian churches claim to believe in the Trinity (God is one Being expressed in three persons), finding out how a particular church perceives God the Holy Spirit may be very enlightening.

The way the Holy Spirit is treated by some churches, he might have an identity crisis if he weren't God! Many churches make him out to be the lesser of the three persons of God, and some even go so far as to suggest that the Holy Spirit is not part of the deity at all. The Bible is very clear on this matter—and you should seek a church that is very clear on it as well. (Acts 5:3-4; 2 Corinthians 3:18)

The Holy Spirit has the same attributes as God and Jesus Christ—he is eternal, omnipresent, omnipotent, and omniscient. It is surprising how many churches shortchange the Holy Spirit. (Psalm 139:7-10; Luke 1:35; 1 Corinthians 2:10-11; Hebrews 9:14)

What does the Holy Spirit do? The Bible outlines at least five areas of activity that the Spirit is engaged in. One of the primary tasks of the Holy Spirit is to help the nonbeliever come to faith in Christ: "When he [the Holy Spirit] comes, he will convict the world of guilt in regard to sin." (John 16:8; see also 3:3-8; Titus 3:5) We read in the Scriptures that the Holy Spirit lives within believers: "Do you not know that your body is a temple of the Holy Spirit, who is in you, whom you have received from God?" (1 Corinthians 6:19; see also, Romans 8:9); guarantees the eternal life of the believer (Ephesians 1:13-14); gives us the power that we need to resist sin and have victory over evil (Romans 8); and is responsible for the anointing of believers for knowledge, teaching, and service. (1 Corinthians 12:41; John 2:27)

Along with all of the pleasant things we receive from our relationship with the Holy Spirit, we need to recognize that we have a responsibility in the relationship, too. For instance, there are various ways in which our behavior can offend the Holy Spirit. We read in the Bible about grieving the Holy Spirit (Galatians 5:17-19; Ephesians 4:30-31); quenching the Spirit (1 Thessalonians 5:19); blaspheming the Holy Spirit, which is perhaps the most serious sin we can commit, since there is no forgiveness for this offense (Matthew 12:31-32); and resisting the Holy Spirit (Acts 7:51). If a church neither believes nor teaches these matters, its theology is incomplete, and your own spiritual growth will be significantly hindered.

Often, the teaching about "spiritual gifts" is related to the church's beliefs about the Holy Spirit. There is a category of churches—such as the Assemblies of God and Pentecostal churches—which practice the use of the "charismatic" gifts. These are gifts such as speaking in tongues and healing. Depending upon your interpretation of the Bible, and how comfortable you feel in the midst of a charismatic congregation, discovering the congregation's beliefs about charismatic gifts may be a pivotal decision point for you.

Sin and Satan

How does the church deal with the notion of sin? Do we still have to address the residue of the "original sin"—that which was committed by Adam and Eve? Does sin negate our ability to relate to God, to serve him, or to be saved by him? The answers related to sin and forgiveness are critical, since the Christian faith is founded upon the life and death of Jesus Christ to restore us to relationship with God, a restoration made necessary by our sin against God.

Does the church believe in the existence of a being known as Satan or the devil, or does it believe that this character has been developed as merely a symbol of sin and deception? Is there a physical place called hell, or is it simply a state of mind?

Some churches preach about being engaged in "spiritual warfare." Does the church you are visiting perceive any type of on-going spiritual tension between God and Satan, manifested in the lives of people? If the spiritual warfare concept is taught, what does the church promote as the solution to that warfare? The Bible suggests that this warfare is real, and is existent today, and that we can be assured of victory. Does the church you are visiting acknowledge that warfare and prepare its people to win the battle, or does it leave them defenseless in combat?

Salvation

How can men and women be saved from eternal damnation if they have sinned against a holy and righteous God? This question has caused many divisions between churches, and is responsible for the formation of a number of new denominations and sects.

Different churches combine aspects of faith, repentance, baptism, acceptance of Jesus as Savior, predestination, good works, and priestly sanction into a doctrine of salvation. What does salvation mean to the church, and how can a person gain salvation? Since the forgiveness of our sins, and the hope of eternal life with Christ in heaven is the ultimate aim of our life on earth, it is important to know what the church believes about salvation.

The Bible

Most Christian churches will agree that the Bible is central to their teaching and activity. However, not all Christian churches teach that the Bible is *the* central authority. Not all Christian churches teach that the

Bible is the inspired Word of God. And not all Christian
churches teach that the Bible is the inerrant, infallible
Word, written by God through men, to be taken literally
and applied exactly.

The Sacraments

Sacraments are physical representations of God's
grace to mankind. The two sacraments recognized by
most Protestant churches are baptism and the Lord's
Supper.

Baptism is designed to be an outward sign that the
baptized individual has some type of relationship with
Jesus Christ. Here the division starts, however. Some
churches believe in and practice "infant baptism," claim-
ing the young child for God's kingdom, and (in some
churches) establishing the responsibility of the congregation to nurture the child into mature Christian faith.
Other churches conduct a "believer's baptism," explaining that since baptism is to be an outward sign of belief
in Christ and acceptance of him as one's Savior, such can
only have meaning when the individual is old enough to
make an informed decision to follow Christ. Baptism,
then, is the public act of sealing that decision.

There are some churches within the Protestant
tradition that teach the necessity of baptism to be "saved."
This is a controversial teaching since there is an absence
of specific teaching in the Bible that baptism (and not
just faith alone) is needed to gain eternal life.

There are also churches—most of which are charismatic churches—that believe in two baptisms, the
second being a "baptism of the Holy Spirit," at which
time the believer is empowered with special spiritual
gifts through the supernatural workings of the Holy

Spirit. Much of the controversy raised in relation to this focuses upon the assumed incompleteness of a person's Christian faith if he or she has not experienced this second form of baptism.

Non-charismatic churches generally believe that there is a single baptism, which acts as a public witness of one's faith in Jesus Christ. Most non-charismatic churches assert that believers fully receive the Holy Spirit upon accepting Christ as their personal Savior.

The other sacrament practiced by most Protestant churches is the Lord's Supper, also referred to as Communion or the Eucharist. The Lord's Supper entails the symbolic breaking and eating of bread, and the symbolic drinking of wine (or, in many churches, grape juice). This is done in imitation of the "Last Supper," the final dinner which Christ had with his disciples, during which he instructed them to continue that tradition as a means of recalling why he came and why he would soon die.

Churches vary widely on how often they have Communion and who is eligible to participate in the Communion bread and wine. To some churches, the only people eligible to participate in Communion are those who are members of the local congregation; elsewhere, anyone who is a professing Christian is qualified; in other churches, everybody present is invited to join in the Communion celebration. The determination of which approach makes the most sense should be based upon your understanding of what the Lord's Supper was intended, by Christ, to accomplish.

Roles and Responsibilities

Within the workings of the church as an institution, what is the role of the minister? The role of the lay person? What is the responsibility of the church to the person who believes in Jesus Christ and trusts in him for salvation? And what is the role of the church to those in the world who have not accepted Christ as their Redeemer? By answering these questions, you'll learn a lot about the church's perspective on lay ministry, evangelism, and discipleship.

Gaining the Desired Information

Naturally, upon entering a church service on a Sunday morning, there will not be someone at the door waiting to answer your theological and doctrinal questions about the church. To get the answers to your questions, you may have to do some digging.

Most churches have an information packet prepared for visitors, and some of your questions will undoubtedly be answered by that packet. The packet will also provide additional information about the church that it considers to be important to a visitor. Reflect on what information they have chosen to provide. This, in itself, offers a telltale insight into where the church places its emphasis, and what it may hold to be the most important elements of the church.

If you are attentive during the Sunday service you attend, you will also pick up other clues about the church's beliefs and practices. Listen to the prayers, and the language used in the prayers, as indicators of how the church understands God's relationship to man.

Observing the rituals and activities that take place during the service will help show you how much importance the church places on tradition and symbolism, and how it views the role of lay people in the church's worship of God. The sermon will provide substantial insight into the church's theological bent. Notice how often, and in what ways, passages from the Bible are used—to justify a position, to point the way to a position, to satisfy people's need to feel that the church is based upon Scripture, and so forth.

Consider how the music is integrated into the service, and the content of that music. Check the bulletin to determine the titles of the people who take part in the service, toward understanding their view of authority, hierarchy, team ministry, and the like. You can also consult the bulletin or other church literature to learn more about the focus of the church programs. All of these aspects of the Sunday service can further enlighten you in ways which may not be conveyed through literature or other means.

Finally, if you have additional questions about the church's beliefs, and are interested in learning more, you should make an appointment to visit with one of the staff members of the church. (If the church has multiple pastors, don't be dismayed if you cannot meet with the senior pastor. That would be the equivalent of your going to Sears and, before applying for a Sears charge card, asking to meet the Chairman of the Board.) During your meeting, which could be by telephone or in person, ask about the things that are on your mind. If elements of the worship service did not make sense to you, ask why they took place, and what their theological significance was. Remember, you are embarking on a significant commitment. Getting the proper information upon which to make a choice is critical. Most church representatives will be happy to answer your questions (and if they are *not*, that should tell you something).

Many churches offer a class for those who wish to find out what the church believes and what church membership involves. There is usually no obligation to those who take the class (although there is the implicit assumption that anyone who attends the sessions is strongly interested in joining the church). These classes are another means of learning about the church and its beliefs. It is suggested that before you make your final determination of what church would be best for you, enroll in one of those classes, to gain the full benefit of knowledge about the church.

A Time Saver

You may be able to pare down your potential list of questions by determining what you can about a church's beliefs prior to your visit. If a church belongs to one of the major denominations, the basic beliefs of the church can be readily determined. (The next chapter discusses denominations, and how some of the larger ones differ from each other.) You may find, for instance, that some churches you had planned to visit do not believe that the Bible is the only reliable source of guidance about Christ, salvation, and other pivotal spiritual matters. If you strongly disagree with this perspective, and hold it to be central to your choice of a church, you may be able to eliminate some churches from the running before expending your time on a visit.

5
So Many Denominations

Before you get too far into your church evaluation experience, you will notice that there is an overwhelming number of different church denominations within the Christian world. In America today, there are more than two hundred different Protestant denominations, each with its own distinct theology, system of government, economic structure, and leadership. Some denominations have been in existence for several hundred years; others have been launched within the past five years. Some denominations are made up of literally thousands of churches, while others have less than a dozen. A few of the better-known denominations have more than five million members, while there are some lesser-known denominations that have fewer than five hundred members in all of their churches combined.

An overview of the role of denominations in church policy and beliefs may offer valuable guidance in your thinking about which churches might best satisfy your needs.

Why Denominations Exist

It might seem foolish to you that a local church would forfeit its autonomy and peculiar identity to join with other churches to form a united body, called a denomination. You might also question the wisdom of attempting to promote personal growth through an an organizational structure that is likely to encourage the depersonalization of the local institution.

And yet, there are a number of valid reasons underlying the "urge to merge" among churches. For instance, there is a certain appeal to being united with other congregations that share the same spiritual beliefs, making more tangible the unity and brotherhood of Christ. There is also a confidence gained from numbers, where people feel bolder and more open about their faith if they know that many other people share their beliefs.

Much of the historical reason behind the existence of denominations is, in fact, related to the desire to promote specific spiritual beliefs which differed from those held by other churches and denominations. In some cases, the differences were more related to styles of worship or methods of church government than to beliefs. However, the motivation in the majority of cases was to be able to worship and believe as they saw fit, without restriction.

Denominations also enable those members who have scholarly inclinations to work together toward strengthening the faith of those within their churches. They could, for instance, put together a "statement of faith," a declaration and explanation of beliefs, serving those on the outside looking in, as well as those within the denomination who are seeking to better understand their own beliefs.

There are also substantial economies of scale to be exploited through such a spiritual association. Consider the heightened political clout when a larger group of churches speaks as one body, and government officials realize that the group represents hundreds, if not thousands, of churches, and thousands upon thousands of adult members. Think about the potential ministry impact that can be achieved through cooperative economics. For instance, some denominations receive a small percentage of each member church's budget to be used for specified missions projects. Although the actual contribution from any single church is minimal, and could accomplish relatively little of its own accord, the aggregate impact can (and has been known to) literally transform a nation's standard of living.

And many denominations have learned that there are great efficiencies (both economic and philosophic) derived through the mass production of materials by the denomination (e.g., Sunday-school materials, books). Indeed, many churches opt to purchase teaching aides developed and produced by their denomination because those materials are targeted to the particular beliefs which their denomination, alone, may promote. Many churches also take advantage of the volume discounts when purchasing goods and services available from external sources (e.g., retirement plans, insurance coverage, Bibles).

Denominations can offer the advantages of a shared vision managed and sharpened by individuals capable of providing leadership to more than just a single church. While the minister of a local church might have strengths in visiting people in the community, or preaching relevant messages every Sunday, he may have little understanding of, or no talent for more technical matters such as organizational structure, or the articulation of a broad-

based vision for ministry. The denominational affiliation, however, would enable a local minister to build
upon a structure and vision developed, tested, and
refined by the denomination, thereby allowing the
minister to concentrate and capitalize upon his own
areas of strength.

From a marketing perspective, there are still other
benefits to be gained through joining together. It's
similar to the concept of a franchise, like McDonald's or
Pizza Hut. Through cooperative advertising, more
people can be reached more efficiently with advertising
and promotions. It may also be easier for a church to
grow in size if it belongs to a denomination which has a
solid history, high name recognition, and high credibil-
ity. The local "franchise" can, to some degree, ride on
the coattails of the denomination.

The interviews conducted with church members
around the country underscored the importance of the
denominational connection, especially when people have
to relocate from one area to another. "I looked for a
church in the same denomination as my old church,"
explained one middle-aged woman whose husband
was transferred from the Northeast to a smaller community in the Midwest. "Even though I didn't know anybody in the town, I knew what the denomination's
beliefs were, and felt that checking out their local church
might make matters easier. At least I didn't have to
worry about them teaching things that I didn't believe
in."

The Major Players

Of course, there are some who maintain that things
have gotten out of hand, asserting that there is no need

for the 229 denominations known to exist in America today. Even so, we can learn much about church selection by noting which denominations are the most widespread.

First, there is the distinction between Protestant and Catholic churches. About three out of ten American adults consider themselves to be Roman Catholic, and are affiliated with one of the twenty-three thousand Catholic churches in this country. About six out of ten adults are self-described Protestants, and attend one of the three hundred thousand known Protestant churches.

It is within the Protestant group of churches that the phenomenon of denominationalism is at work. Over the course of the past two hundred years, things have become so splintered within the Protestant community that even within some of the major denominations there have been divisions, creating new denominations from within the old. On the next page is a list of the largest Protestant denominations, and how many congregations and church members each currently has.

One important aspect to highlight is that calling a church "Baptist" or "Methodist" or by any other "generic" name may be misleading. There are more than a dozen denominations affiliated with the Baptist faith, for instance. Although they all have some principles of faith and practice in common, there are certain matters on which they have significant distinctions. Be careful in how you think and talk about churches, realizing that you need to know the specific denominational affiliation (e.g., Lutheran—Missouri Synod, rather than simply Lutheran) to have an accurate understanding of some of the church's beliefs.

Interestingly, although there are 229 denominations in America, the twenty-three listed on the chart (less than 10 percent of all the denominations) contain

Denomination	Congregations	Members*	
Southern Baptist Convention	37,072	14,613,618	
United Methodist Church	37,876	9,192,172	
National Baptist Convention, USA	26,000	5,500,000	(1958)
Evangelical Lutheran Church in America	11,127	5,300,000	
Church of God in Christ	9982	3,709,661	
Presbyterian Church (USA)	11,531	3,007,322	
National Baptist Convention of America	11,398	2,668,799	(1956)
Lutheran Church—Missouri Synod	5897	2,630,588	
Episcopal Church	7054	2,504,507	
African Methodist Episcopal	6200	2,210,000	
Assemblies of God	10,886	2,135,104	
United Church of Christ	6406	1,676,105	
Churches of Christ	13,364	1,623,754	
American Baptist	5864	1,576,483	
Baptist Bible Fellowship	3449	1,405,900	
African Methodist Episcopal Zion	6057	1,195,173	
Christian Church (Disciples of Christ)	4221	1,106,692	
Christian Church/Church of Christ	5566	1,063,469	
Christian Methodist Episcopal Church	2340	718,922	
Church of the Nazarene	5018	530,912	
Progressive National Baptist Convention	655	521,692	(1967)
Church of God (Cleveland, Tenn.)	5346	505,775	
United Pentecostal Church, International	3410	500,000	

*Source (except for Evangelical Lutheran Church in America): Constant Jacquet, Jr., ed., *Yearbook of American and Canadian Churches 1988* (Nashville: Abingdon Press, 1988). Membership figures are for 1981 or later, except where noted.

more than three-quarters of all the Protestant churches in the nation. The people who attend the churches in those twenty-three denominations constitute better than two out of every three adults affiliated with a Protestant church. In other words, if you want to know how most people worship, and where they choose to affiliate spiritually, your best bet would be to study churches associated with these denominations.

Again, a caution: These churches are not the only game in town, and recent statistics show that some of the fastest growing denominations—another indicator of healthy, need-satisfying churches—are those which have not yet reached the proportions that would get them on such a list.

Many of the fastest-growing churches are non-denominational churches, or smaller, conservative denominations. These churches span the gamut in the nature of their beliefs and in forms of government. Don't overlook some of these churches as possibilities. In many of the communities I have visited, it is the non-denominational churches that are the most exciting and vibrant congregations to be found.

Some Differences in Beliefs

As was mentioned earlier, one of the motivations for starting a new denomination is often the need to espouse a distinctive set of spiritual beliefs. In some cases, the distinctions are what the average person might consider to be "splitting hairs." In other cases, the differences might constitute a major theological divergence.

It is not the purpose of this book to define the theological positions of the major denominations on a series of issues and doctrines deemed to be significant. Rather, it is my hope to sensitize you to the fact that there are significant differences between the denominations, and to help you figure out which, if any, of those differences matter in your decision of what church to embrace. In that light, what follows is simply an overview of a few areas in which some of the major denominations have different perspectives.

A. Views About the Bible

A major difference exists between Protestant and Catholic churches, generally, on the Bible. Protestants utilize a Bible which contains sixty-six books, as recognized by church scholars and leaders in the fourth century A.D. The Roman Catholic Church uses a Bible that includes the same sixty-six books, plus an additional seven known as the Apocrypha. Protestants do not recognize those seven books as truly inspired by God, although they are used for historical insight.

Protestant churches generally believe that the interpretation of the Bible is the prerogative of the individual, with the clergy assisting in the analysis of passages for more accurate perspectives. Roman Catholics, on the other hand, believe that the leaders of the Catholic Church itself have been divinely appointed to pass along the true interpretation of the Bible for the people. Although individuals are encouraged to read the Bible and apply its teachings in their lives, the more important decisions on interpretation are made by the Catholic hierarchy in Rome.

Protestant churches have adopted what scholars refer to as conservative and liberal positions pertaining to the use and interpretation of the Bible. Conservatives, such as the Southern Baptist Convention, Lutheran Church (Missouri Synod), and Presbyterian Church in America, teach that the Bible was written by God, through selected men, and is to be treated as a precise statement of reality and direction for behavior and belief (in religious circles, these churches are said to believe in the "inerrancy" of Scripture). They view the Bible as the highest authority for church teaching and practice. The role of the individual is to consult Scripture in all matters, and to interpret the Bible in light of the context of the teaching and the principles it reveals.

Other churches, such as the Episcopal, Presbyterian Church (USA), and United Methodists, believe that the Bible is an inspired book, providing the principles by which God would have us live, but that it is not necessarily to be followed word for word. They submit that, due to differences in aspects such as the accuracy of the translation and the social context of the interpretation, the Bible ought to act as a major guiding force, but not as the sole authority.

Still other churches consider factors such as human reason, personal leading from God, experience, and tradition to be integral to their treatment of what the Bible says.

B. Salvation

The issue of salvation was the wedge that divided the Roman Catholic Church some five hundred years ago, giving birth to what we know today as the various Protestant faiths. The Catholic church teaches that eternal salvation is dispensed by God to those whom he chooses to reward for their good behavior and their faith in him. It says that men cannot know, prior to their judgment experience, whether or not they will receive eternal salvation.

Most Protestant churches, on the other hand, assert that people receive salvation through the act of submission in faith to Jesus Christ as their Savior. While good works are considered one of the manifestations of one's faith, they are not a necessary ingredient to gain salvation. The key factors are acknowledgment of our sin, and the acceptance of God as our spiritual Father, and Jesus Christ as our Redeemer from sin and damnation.

Churches have varying interpretations of the Bible's teaching about predestination. Many churches, such as those in the Presbyterian category, believe that God has predetermined whether or not a person will be spared eternal damnation. They nevertheless believe that the individual has the responsibility to choose whether or not to accept the gift of salvation that is reserved for, and available to the "elect." Other bodies, such as the Baptists, believe that all people have the opportunity to accept Christ as their Savior and thus be brought into God's everlasting kingdom.

There are even different views on what constitutes salvation, with some churches emphasizing the future aspect—eternal life with God in heaven—while others see salvation as a condition of heightened well-being during this life.

C. *Baptism*

Baptism has become a controversial matter within religious circles. There are churches that believe in baptizing infants (Methodists, Presbyterians, Catholics, Lutherans). Others will only baptize people who are old enough to knowingly profess Christ as their Lord and

Savior (Baptists, Disciples of Christ).

To some denominations, baptism is necessary to receive salvation (Episcopalians, Lutherans). To others, baptism is an outward symbol of an inward change, but is not necessary for salvation (Presbyterians, Baptists, Methodists).

Even the method of baptism has stirred differences. The most common forms are by sprinkling (Congregationalists, Presbyterians, Methodists) and immersion (Baptists, Disciples of Christ).

D. Social Issues and Involvement

Many churches suggest that their people have a special responsibility to be a light to the world by becoming actively involved in the social issues of the day. The distinction between those churches, however, relates to their "official" positions on those issues, and how earnestly they encourage members to become involved.

The Catholic Church has been widely known as one of the more active denominations related to social issues. It has taken stands pertaining to abortion, divorce, AIDS, apartheid, communism, and birth control, among other issues. Catholics are expected to follow the positions set forth by the church, as an act of obedience. A number of Protestant churches have also become activists in specific areas, notably Lutherans and Presbyterians, although involvement is not viewed as an obligation tied to one's spiritual standing.

Some denominations hold that the role of the church is to introduce people to Christ as their Savior, and participation in social causes is left to the discretion of the individual. Churches in this camp often recommend to their members that the Bible be used as the guide to developing a perspective.

There are also some issues which have caused denominations that otherwise would not have been publicly involved to take a stand. Abortion has been a galvanizing issue for Southern Baptists, for instance, on the grounds that it is not simply a social issue but a moral issue clearly addressed by the Bible.

Differences in Structure

Another distinguishing characteristic of denominations is the organizational structure or government that is utilized by member churches. There are three basic forms of government: episcopalian (a hierarchy in which authority is vested in bishops); presbyterian (a multi-tiered system in which the congregation chooses elders to act as their representatives); and congregational (in which local pastors have the overall responsibility for the governance of the church, with assistance from deacons). The names of these forms of government should not be confused with the names of the denominations.

Churches using the episcopal form of government include Catholic, Episcopal, Methodist, and some Lutheran bodies. The Presbyterian Church is the best-known denomination using the form of government that bears its name. Congregational government can be found among the Assemblies of God, most Baptist, Disciples of Christ, and Evangelical Free churches.

These differences are important insofar as they help determine what an individual can and cannot do within the church.

The Reality of Denominations

Suppose you were to drive your car from New York to Los Angeles. Each night, you stopped for dinner at the same fast food restaurant chain, and checked in at motels that were part of the same chain. Undoubtedly, you would find that there were differences in service, pricing, and quality at each location, even though all of the restaurants and motels were supposedly related by the same policies and standards, as established by the organizational headquarters.

Each of the churches that belong to the same denomination probably have much in common. They subscribe to the guiding beliefs and principles of the denomination, but they may not look or act like a carbon copy of every other church in the denomination. Why? Because they are the sum of the people that comprise the local church body, and people are different. Every local congregation takes on its own personality, regardless of the standards and policies set by the denomination. In some ways, then, just as you cannot always judge a book by its cover, you cannot always judge a local church by its denominational affiliation.

You will find that some churches are overtly denominational, constantly informing or reminding you that this is the way churches in the denomination do things. Other bodies are more subtle, almost covert in their displays of denominational behavior and thinking. Ultimately, it is a matter of style which you must study and choose among.

Also recognize that a growing proportion of the churches in America are not affiliated with any denomination. This is likely related to the growing uneasiness which Americans have with associating with larger, umbrella organizations. While it may be somewhat more difficult to get a clear perspective on the history, beliefs, and government of non-denominational churches, do not automatically exclude them from your investigation.

6
How Do They Worship?

The word "worship" is used almost two hundred times in the Bible. The very first of the Ten Commandments which God gave to Moses for the people of Israel addressed their need to worship the God of Creation, and no other gods. During Jesus' time of fasting in the wilderness, before he began his public ministry, Satan tempted him to sin against God by offering him challenges and possessions. The final temptation was the offer of a trade: Satan would give Jesus all the kingdoms of this world if Jesus would just bow down and worship him. Jesus' reply was "you shall worship the Lord your God and Him only you shall serve." (Matthew 4:10, NKJV)

Worship is central to the life of a Christian church. It is a pivotal function which we are commanded to perform, with the proper heart and attitude. For centuries church leaders have recognized this, as described in the Westminster Catechism's description of the role of mankind: to glorify God and enjoy him forever.

Our worship of God helps build our relationship with him. In your exploration of churches, the numerous styles of worship will be among the most obvious and most important determinants of your ultimate choice.

The bottom line is this: Any group of people that convenes for religious purposes, but does not *worship* God, is not a church. As you look for the best church for your needs, do not minimize the critical importance of the ways in which the congregation worships God, and your own experience of that time spent in worship.

The word "worship" is derived from a pair of Old English words which mean "worthship"—that is, any set of thoughts and practices which indicate the value and worthiness of a particular object or being.

The Hebrew language uses two words for "worship." The first is best defined as "bowing down." To worship, in this sense, means to show profound respect, humility, and deference for God. It indicates a deep awareness of God's significance. The second Hebrew term can be described as "service"—a behavioral manifestation of our praise for the living God, offered not out of a sense of obligation but from a heart overflowing with love and gratitude. Taken together, we can therefore understand worship as our response to God's demonstration of his love and power in our lives.

Sociologists who have studied the nature of religious worship have discovered that worship entails four elements: reflection and meditation on the deity, interaction with divinely-derived truth, a conscious and personal encounter with God, and some change of perspective or lifestyle as a result of the worship experience.

One pastor has described the church worship experience as a combination of three factors: truth, taste, and tradition. Every worship service has been designed with certain values in mind that are related to each of those factors. Truth can be seen through the meaning behind the practices and the ideas communicated through readings, prayers, and sermons. Taste accounts for the personality of the church that is revealed through the service. Tradition is represented in some manner through the form and philosophy of the worship service. Some churches choose to replace some of the traditional styles of worship with a contemporary, unique approach, while others prefer to maintain the time-honored traditions handed down to them.

The task facing you, as you search for the church best able to address your needs, is to clarify in your own mind just what you are seeking in terms of a worship experience. In other words, to you, what is truth in worship, what is taste in worship, and what worship traditions have meaning and significance to you?

Styles of Worship

As you evaluate various worship services, there may be four specific aspects which you could consider.

The first of those is whether the church is based upon highly structured, traditional forms of worship, or upon a more modern, flexible approach. The former approach is often called "high church," since it takes a high view of the importance of tradition. This approach centers upon the repetition of prayers, affirmations, and other expressions developed by the church's forerunners. Churches in the Catholic and Episcopalian denominations are examples of the high-church approach. The services change little from week to week, and emphasize tradition rather than creativity in worship.

The "low-church" style of worship is perhaps best expressed in churches affiliated with the Assemblies of

God. In many churches that take this approach, the format changes from week to week, incorporating some new and some old, geared toward creative expression more than the security of tradition. The styles of music, the form of the message, and even the order of the elements within the service might change.

As you experience such shifts in style, you need to determine whether you derive more from the traditional or from the contemporary approach to worship. Do you understand and grow from responsive readings based upon writings of the early pioneers of the church, or do you prefer the more modern expressions written by the church staff specially for this week's service? Is your ability to experience God and worship him enhanced by the singing of the traditional church hymns, accompanied by the pipe organ and choir, or are you more likely to feel God's presence when singing contemporary Christian songs with the accompaniment of a band or piano? These and related questions can only be answered by you—and you can perhaps answer them confidently only after you have experienced both styles of worship.

A second consideration relates to the music contained within the worship service. Above, I alluded to the different types of songs that are sung by churches. Some people find it difficult to wrestle any meaning out of hymns written hundreds of years ago, containing unfamiliar expressions. Others find it nearly impossible to gain a sense of majesty and spirituality from the upbeat "praise" songs penned by some of today's church musicians.

The very sound itself can influence your worship experience. For instance, some of the people we interviewed for this book stated that they dislike the pipe organs and the choir ensembles that characterize so many churches because those forms bear no relationship to the styles of music with which they are comfortable, those that they hear daily on the radio or sing in the shower. Other people indicated that they could not get inspired to worship without the full sound of the organ, and the encouragement of the choir behind them. Again, it is a matter of personal preference and comfort.

The third aspect to consider is the nature of the message communicated by the worship leader. There are several schools of thought related to the best approach to a sermon. Some ministers see their role as primarily that of a teacher, and approach their job as a college professor might. They prepare a lesson in which they seek to impart factual information for the audience to digest and act upon. Another school of thought holds that the role of the minister is to preach directly from the Bible. In this approach, the minister is charged with the task of explaining, exhorting, and encouraging people based upon a strict interpretation of the words in the chosen text. The sermon ought to lead people to reflect upon a situation, consider the biblical basis for action, and respond in an appropriate way. Yet another approach is simply to lead people to reflect upon God, and to actively work on their personal relationship with him through that act of meditation. Other pastors assume a more energetic and upbeat tack, turning the worship service into a time of celebration, where the emphasis is not so much on intellectual growth as upon an emotional experience with God.

While worship strategies differ, none is more proper than another. Each is likely to result in a different outcome for you, the person attending the service. Once again, it all boils down to your expectations of a worship service, and what approach provides you with the most satisfying and fulfilling experience.

Finally, there are large disparities in terms of the amount of participation expected or allowed of people in the congregation. In many churches, the participation consists of singing and perhaps some responsive readings. In other churches, there are other opportunities for sharing prayers of request or thanksgiving. Some churches have a time in which the people present are expected to mingle with each other, and express God's love through the welcoming of each other. There are numerous variations on worship participation. What types of expression and involvement would make your worship experience most real to you?

Outcomes

It is important that you approach your church-selection adventure with a defined sense of what you expect to get from a worship service. Many people are most interested in the opportunity to personally express themselves to God during the service, whether that be through song, through silent prayer, or through dedicated concentration upon him. Many people feel that the church has provided a successful worship service only if they are able to leave the church sanctuary having had a personal encounter with God, in which they affirmed and advanced their personal relationship with the living God.

What does worship mean to you? What do you expect a church worship service to provide to facilitate your worship of God?

Remember that worship, although done in a public forum, is an intensely private experience. Nobody can tell you whether or not you truly worshiped God, and nobody can tell you exactly how to derive the most appropriate and deepest worship experience. But as you search for a church, keep in mind that the centerpiece of the typical church, and the aspect around which the church life typically revolves, is the worship service. If a church provided you with no other benefit than the opportunity to experience a growing relationship with God through the worship time, that church would have served a laudable function.

Worship: Useful, but Necessary?

One of the aspects of worship that many churches lose over time is the element of joy. Can you imagine a more exciting, a more fulfilling, or a more joyful experience than being in the presence of God, developing a stronger and more intimate relationship with him? Unfortunately, some churches treat the worship service like a routine chore, something that must be done every Sunday or else! There is no sense of being uplifted by the worship experience, no enhancement of the bonding with our heavenly Father and with Jesus Christ our Redeemer. Indeed, some might question whether those services, regardless of the name given to them, are truly *worship* services.

One insight that I picked up from my own exploration of churches is that the factor that makes all the difference is the *attitude* of the church toward worship. In a church which has a truly transforming, transcendent worship service, the focus is upon God—not upon the speaker, the singers, the ushers, or anything else. The criterion for judging the worship service is not the number of people who show up, or the brilliance of the sermon or solos, but the ability of participants to experience God.

Is worship critical to finding the right church, even if you have never felt the importance of the worship experience, never felt a special uplifting through worship? Absolutely! God clearly commands us, in the Bible, to place a premium upon worship. It is the foundation of our relationship with him. As such, worship ought to be the highlight of our week, a highly personal expression of our enjoyment of God in our lives. A church that enables you to know God in that intimate way, and to continue to grow closer to him through worship, is a church worthy of very serious consideration.

7
Forming New Relationships

"I moved to this city, not knowing anybody. When I visited this church, it was the first time that I really started to feel like I belonged in this area. The people accepted me, and almost all of my real friends are members of this church."

Those were the words of a woman who moved to a new home in a different part of the country. A committed Christian, what brought comfort and meaning to her new home was not the salary increase her husband received, nor the larger home they were able to purchase. It was the chance to meet people who loved her and cared about her because she, too, was committed to Jesus Christ.

God made people as social beings and expects us to have meaningful relationships with each other. It is through those relationships that we find fulfillment in life, and come to know ourselves better. It is often through our relationships with others that we also come to know more about God and his relationship with us.

God's plan for the Christian church was that it

should become a means for like-minded people to meet each other, encourage each other, educate each other, and enjoy each other. In the midst of a fast-paced and selfish world, where many of the things that Christians believe and cherish are scorned by others, the church becomes our sanctuary.

But God did not intend for the church to become a hiding place where we can practice piety in secret before rejoining the world on its own terms. The church was designed to be a place where believers could worship, study, celebrate, relax, and regain their strength, partially in anticipation of being able to confront the world with the truth about Christ. The preparation for that involvement in the world includes mutual encouragement and genuine enjoyment of the friendship of others who have the same spiritual perspective.

If you read about the early church in Acts, you find that the followers of the risen Christ took their faith so seriously that they were willing to leave their natural families in order to be united with other people who held the same spiritual beliefs and commitment. The church of the first century was truly an extended family, in which people pooled their possessions, lived and traveled together, and spent a great part of their time enabling each other to advance in their faith.

That kind of kinship seems very remote to us today. In America in these waning years of the twentieth century, the pressures and challenges we face every day seem almost to prohibit, rather than foster, the development of any type of close relationships with anyone outside our immediate family. In fact, it is not even easy to hold our families together.

Sociologists inform us that one of the consequences of our rushed, fast-lane lifestyles, complete with all the latest advances in technology, is a sense of loneliness unparalleled in this century. Rather than becoming a nation of people seeking to grow together, we have become a country of nomads who change locations frequently, isolate ourselves from others thanks to the miracles of entertainment technology (satellite television, VCRs, personal computers, etc.), and spend less and less time interacting with other human beings.

For some people, this is a tragic development, causing more suicides than we have seen at any other time in the nation's history. At the very least, the social changes we have encountered have turned us into a pack of loners—interested in bonding with other people, but not quite sure how to do so, and unfamiliar with ways and places in which such relationships might be forged.

The Christian church offers a solution to the aloneness that so many are seeking to escape. Even for those who have a robust social life, the church represents a means of being with other people who share common interests and needs.

Not surprisingly, then, our research discovered that many people were attracted to a church because of the possibility of meeting new people and becoming part of a group with similar interests, concerns, or backgrounds. Other research has shown that most new church members first attended those churches because they were invited to do so by someone whom they knew and trusted. Further, we learned that one of the most compelling reasons people identified for sticking with their current church was that their friends—many of whom they met only after becoming active at the church—were also members of that church. To these people, the church had become a part of their extended family.

In the previous chapter we examined some aspects

of worship—the activities that enable you to initiate and nurture your relationship with God. For a church to provide a whole ministry, though, its activities, programs, and structures must promote the building of solid relationships between people.

When you visit a church, try to answer this question: Is the focus of the ministry on satisfying the spiritual and personal needs of the *people*, or upon the development and numerical success of the *programs* that are offered to the people? At first, the difference may not be evident to you, but it is a difference worth trying to ascertain.

I have attended one too many churches whose intentions were great, but whose efforts were ill-placed. Ideally, a church will concentrate on bringing people together, and encouraging people to invest themselves in the lives and struggles of other people toward making them whole. Instead, many churches emphasize making their programs work, which either means having a certain number of people involved, or viewing the program as an end in itself, rather than a means to an end. The churches which I have found to be most valuable to my own maturation—both in my Christian faith, and in my personality—have been those which paid more attention to who I am and what I need, than to what programs I can be plugged into.

Clues About Relationships

The only way to really know how easy it will be to form meaningful relationships with the people attending a church is to spend time in their midst, and see what develops. To get some early indications, however, here are a few signs you can look for.

The high point of most church experiences is the Sunday-morning program. This probably includes a worship service and the availability of Sunday-school classes. This is also the time when the greatest number of church members are present. You can learn a lot simply by observing a few things.

First, has the church made an effort to allow people to have contact with each other and to develop friendships? Some churches accomplish this by having a time within the worship service itself when people introduce themselves to others seated nearby, in the hope that this will facilitate further interaction after the service. Some churches have special means of identifying visitors, and enabling church members to welcome them personally.

Also carefully watch how much interaction there is between the people in the church. In some congregations, you would think you were attending a funeral, if you didn't know better, because the mood is solemn, and the personal touch is wholly missing. In other congregations, you'd think you were attending a wedding celebration, because the mood is so upbeat and sincerely joyous.

Observe the interaction that takes place between services and in the Sunday-school classes. What to look for depends upon what you feel you would be most comfortable with: a low-key approach to building relationships, or a more aggressive style of interacting.

Another indicator of the likelihood that you will have a positive experience at the church in building relationships concerns the demographics of the congregation. I have talked with hundreds of people around the country about their churches, and their frustrations with the church. One frustration that consistently emerges is the lack of a sufficient number of people who are of a similar age and background. One of the social realities of Americans is that, even if we are not prejudiced against people of different backgrounds, we don't always feel comfortable about getting to know people who are quite different from us.

Age, in particular, seems to be a major obstacle to bringing people together. Young people have nothing against older adults, or vice versa, but there is often a lack of easy grounds for conversation. Many people fear that others will not be able to relate to their own struggles and joys, because their experiences are not the same. (I have found this to be especially common among people who participate in a small Bible study group comprised of both young and older adults; the sharing of applications and struggles is often strained or disjointed because of the very different lifestyles and circumstances represented.) To a lesser extent, there are other social class distinctions that might limit your ability to find a comfortable social niche within a given church.

This assessment is especially important if you come from a circumstance that is foreign to the traditional church experience—such as being a divorced single parent, or being part of a racially-mixed marriage, or a naturalized citizen. The sad truth is that some churches are not very tolerant and accepting of people who are different than they are. Whether their approach is right or wrong may not even be the issue for you, as you study the feasibility of becoming part of that body. The reality with which you must deal is whether or not you can reasonably expect to be embraced as an equal and important part of that particular church family, given your circumstances.

Another clue will be how you are treated after your visit. Many churches have systems in place to assist visitors in feeling welcome, and to help integrate them into the church. You might receive a personal visit at

your home by the pastor or some other church represen-
tative. You might receive a telephone call. Perhaps the
church will mail you a letter, thanking you for your
attendance and inviting you to return as soon and as
often as possible. Or, maybe, you will not hear from the
church. You can partially gauge how important you
were to the church based upon whether or not they
made any effort to contact you. And you can pick up
other useful information about the church through your
conversation with its representatives.

Hard-to-Get Information

The types of insights just suggested may be obtained through observation and experience during (or
shortly after) your visit. There are other indicators of
how relationships within the church work which may
take some digging to discover.

If you can get a realistic response, it is sometimes
helpful to know the facts about the actual growth of the
church. A congregation that is growing by leaps and
bounds is very likely satisfying the felt needs of people,
whether those are social, spiritual, or both. A church
that is either stable in its membership, or suffering from
a loss of members, may warrant extra careful scrutiny.
There is always a reason behind that declining performance, and you should be careful to evaluate why this is
happening. In some cases, the reason is not that which
the leaders of the church believe it to be. Based upon
your own judgment of what is happening with the size
of the membership, consider whether or not that is a
warning for you to be cautious about your involvement
with that church.

You might also try to gain some insight into the

proportion of people who are truly involved in the church. Realistically, most churches are described by the 80-20 principle: 80 percent of the work is accomplished by just 20 percent of the people. What you need to be particularly sensitive to are those churches in which just a handful of people, maybe even less than 20 percent, ever participate in church activities. This includes evangelism, socials, worship preparation, Bible-study groups, and the like. If people attend the Sunday-morning services, but put no additional effort into the church, the chances are better than even that you will find it a difficult place in which to form meaningful and lasting relationships.

Check out a calendar of church events. This, too, will help round out your perspective on how important the church leaders consider relationships to be. If the church does not have an agenda which promotes social gatherings and other means of getting to know and support each other, then you need to find out exactly how the church *does* promote relationships.

Most churches offer adult Sunday-school classes that you can attend, usually before or after the main worship service. Often, this is a more relaxed and intimate setting. In my own experience, it has been largely through the Sunday-school classes that I have gotten to know people, the ministers, and the general workings of the church. Visiting one or more of the Sunday-school classes may give you a better handle on how much time and effort it will take to become integrated into the church.

A series of research studies we have conducted during the past several years have shown that perhaps the single most effective way for people to make significant friendships within the church body is through small groups. The objective of the groups varies from church to church, and sometimes from group to group within the same church.

Generally, there are three aspects which the groups seek to satisfy: studying the Bible, praying to thank God for his blessings and to offer personal requests for future blessings, and spending time getting to know the other members of the group. The groups typically consist of anywhere between six and twenty people, and meet once a week, or every other week, usually in the home of one of the group members. Find out if the church has a small group program in operation, and how alive the program is.

General Impressions

After your initial visit to a church, you will probably come away with a general impression of whether or not you think you would be able to break into the social circle of that church, and whether or not the church contains the types of people with whom you would feel comfortable. This is about as much as you might reasonably hope to learn after just a visit or two. The only way to really know if you will be able to develop lasting and meaningful relationships would be to attend the church for an extended period of time and see what develops. Friendships cannot be rushed into existence; any type of interpersonal bonding takes time, enabling the partners to work through the various stages of a friendship. However, do not overlook your first impressions, as they are on target more often than not.

8
Opportunities for Involvement

Let me start off this chapter with a bold statement: Unless you become involved in the activities of your church, you will never truly feel satisfied with that church.

This may seem a bit strong, and may even conflict with your interest in attending a church. The fact is, however, that most people who attend church and feel that the church is inspiring, fulfilling, and adding something special to their lives are the individuals who do more than simply attend services on Sunday mornings. They are characterized by involvement in the practical, ministry activities of the church.

Research has consistently shown that people who merely attend church, without any commitment to participating more actively, find that church becomes a routine, and that it tends not to provide a substantial benefit to their life. Interviews conducted with pastors from all types of churches suggested that one of the reasons why they urge people to take responsibility for some aspect of the church's activity is so they feel like they are truly part of the church family, and come away with a more positive experience.

It seems, then, that the old adage is true: You only get out of a church as much as you put into it. You cannot take, take, take, and take some more, without at some point balancing the relationship and putting something back in.

We even find that the Bible teaches us that we were created by God to serve him, first, and to serve other people, second. One of the most important and efficient means of serving God and others is through the work of the church.

Recall in chapter 6, where we discussed worship, that one of the two facets of worship is service. God takes pleasure in our willingness to do things which further the purposes of the church; he is glorified through our practical involvement in church life.

What happens to people when they play an active role in the church? First, people tell us that the more they get involved, the more they feel that the church is really *their* church, not just any old church that they happen to be attending. They gain a sense of emotional *ownership* of the church because they have invested part of themselves in its health and development.

Second, church participants find that they have an easier time getting to know people who have the same interests. Often, people's friendship circles grow out of their involvement in church work. Many people told us about the new friends they made, and how those relationships were deeper and more meaningful because they were founded upon a common interest in serving the Lord and giving something back to the church.

Third, involvement pushes people to know themselves better. God has given every one of us special talents and skills, described in the Bible as "spiritual gifts." He instilled those in us with the intention that we would use them. People generally find that when they use their gifts for the benefit of the church, not only do they realize personal growth, but they gain the joy of knowing that they have had a positive impact in the lives of others.

Fourth, people who actively do the ministry of the church frequently find that it renews and strengthens their relationship with God, and takes it to new levels. This is because the reason why we do such work is out of our love for God, not out of a feeling of obligation or a need to satisfy peer pressure. We may receive a multitude of benefits from our church service, but the greatest of these may be the special bonding it creates between us and the God we are serving through our efforts.

Remember, the church is the sum of the people who attend and who commit their resources (time, money, talents) to the ministry of that church. If you are interested in getting the most out of a church, you should evaluate the church in light of how effectively it utilizes its people, through their gifts.

Spiritual Gifts

To many people who are seeking a Bible-based church for the first time, the concept of spiritual gifts is new. Let's spend a moment looking at the Bible to get an overview of this area.

Teaching about spiritual gifts varies widely. However, the basic ideas come from three sections of the Bible: Romans 12:6-8;1 Corinthians 12:8-10, 28-30; and Ephesians 4:11.

To help understand where you fit in with this

teaching, perhaps we can divide the gifts described in those passages into three areas: the charismatic gifts; the gifts of character; and the functional gifts.

Charismatic gifts are those such as tongues, interpretation, miracles, and healing. Gifts of character include faith, discernment, wisdom, and knowledge. All of these gifts are important, and can be of considerable service to both the church and to other people. Churches have different ways of understanding the utility of these particular gifts, and if you believe that you possess one or more of those gifts, you should speak to the church leaders to determine exactly how they incorporate those gifts into the church ministry.

The types of gifts of which people are most likely to be aware, and which the church most commonly uses, are the functional gifts. There are two types of functional gifts: those related to communication (evangelism, prophecy, teaching, exhortation, and pastoring) and support gifts (mercy, service, giving, and administration). Here is a brief description of each of the functional gifts:

Evangelism. The purposeful and continual attempt to lead other people to accept Jesus Christ as their Savior.

Prophecy. Proclaiming God's truth by pointing out problem areas in society or in personal lives, and encouraging people to make things right before God.

Teaching. Accurately explaining the intricacies and subtleties of the Bible, making God's truth clear and applicable to the average person.

Exhortation. Practical problem-solving, based upon the Bible. This includes counseling on a wide range of matters.

Pastoring. Overseeing, preparing, and assisting a

group of believers to reach their full potential in Christ; this is accomplished through both teaching and personal relationships, done within the context of spiritual leadership.

Mercy. Providing love, comfort, assurance, and practical assistance to those who need deep understanding and compassion.

Service. Involvement with manual labor and doing logistical and creative tasks that allow ministry to happen.

Giving. Donating material resources to the church and those in need, without seeking any financial or other reimbursement or recognition.

Administration. Accepting responsibility for the planning, implementation, and evaluation of programs and projects, utilizing both people and materials to accomplish specified objectives.

Many people find it difficult to determine their spiritual gifts. Let me suggest three endeavors that may help clarify your gifts:

First, read the Bible passages alluded to above, with respect to spiritual gifts. Examine how the gifts were used in the early church (reading the Book of Acts would be helpful). To help make sense of this area, you may also wish to read respected books or commentaries about spiritual gifts. You will find that some churches do not believe that any of the gifts are operative today, some believe that certain gifts are still available to believers but that others are not, while other congregations believe that every gift is at work in today's Church. Your first step, then, is to become knowledgeable about the gifts and determine what you believe.

Second, pray to God that he will make you aware of your gifts so that you can serve him more effectively.

As you read and learn about the gifts, you will discover that God has endowed every believer with one or more spiritual gift. (1 Corinthians 7:7; 12:7; 1 Peter 4:10)

Third, ask some people who are spiritually mature and know you well what they perceive your gifts to be. Sometimes God uses the wisdom of other people to inform us about things that we may be too close to see. If you feel you know what your gifts are, he may use others to confirm your understanding of God's blessing in your life.

In the end, whether you feel you have a crystal clear sense of your gifts, or are still struggling to narrow down the list of likely possibilities, you need to get involved in the church you choose. Once you try an area in which you think you may be specially gifted, it becomes easier to evaluate whether or not you were right about what your gift is. Remember, regardless of what gift or how many gifts you possess, they are of little value unless you put them to use.

What to Look For

At any church you visit, try to get a sense of the philosophy of the paid staff toward the people who volunteer their time and efforts. In some churches, volunteers are cherished, treated as partners in ministry, on a level that is every bit equal to that of the seminary-trained pastor. Those churches will afford you the greatest opportunity to explore your own gifts, and to experience the joy of growing through helping others.

Some churches, however, have different, less laudable perceptions of volunteers. In some cases it is because the paid staff members feel threatened—as if the volunteers will make their jobs less necessary, and thus undermine the security of their position. In other churches, I have seen staff people treat volunteers more like indentured servants than equals in ministry. In churches where the volunteer is not adequately appreciated and supported by the paid staff, service can be a frustrating experience.

I have seen several churches in which the volunteered assistance of the church members was taken so seriously, and so greatly appreciated, that a special program was designed to ensure that people got the most out of their involvement. Those churches had a series of seminars on discovering one's spiritual gifts, and understanding how those gifts were used within that particular church. The members of those churches with whom I spoke were usually very excited about their involvement, knowing that it mattered to the church and that they themselves were finding their experiences to be gratifying.

It might be a good idea to talk to some of the people who are active in each church you visit, to gain their perspective on what it is like to be involved in ministry in that church. (Sometimes it also helps to get some feedback from people who attend the church regularly, but have chosen not to participate—find out the reasons why they do not get involved, and any past experiences they have had at the church.)

One piece of information you should try to glean is whether the people who are involved really feel that they are making a difference, or if their involvement simply seems like a means of keeping people busy. With the numerous needs existing in every community, and the unique opportunities that churches have to address those needs through well-designed and properly targeted outreach activities, you ought to use your own talents in a church where you have a real chance to impact people's lives.

What does the church require of people before it will allow them to serve? Do you have to be formally accepted as a member of the congregation before they will allow you to take on responsibilities? What are the requirements you must meet before you would be allowed to serve on some of the decision-making boards or committees? For instance, in some churches, any member can serve on a board, if he or she is asked to do so by the appropriate group. In other churches, however, there are longevity requirements, such as having to be a member for five years before being eligible for consideration for a leadership position. Depending upon your background, your talents, and the level of involvement you wish to have, the prerequisites for service may make a big difference in the appeal of a particular church to you.

One of the most important things to look for are signs of volunteer burnout. In many churches, only a handful of members do the bulk of the work. This puts a tremendous strain on those few people, and can lead to ministry fatigue, a state in which the individual no longer has much interest in doing anything related to personal or organizational ministry. Naturally, this condition is antithetical to the very purpose which the church was designed to address.

Churches can avoid volunteer burnout by using strategies designed to take care of the member. For instance, some churches have a wide enough range of options for service that when people become tired of their particular type of involvement, they can shift to another program or type of involvement, rather than give up and get out.

One church I recently visited recognized the importance of being able to count on people's help, but also knew that it had to be realistic about how much it could expect from people. Their solution was to have people make an up-front commitment to a limited duration of specified service (such as six months of teaching the second-grade Sunday-school class), after which the individual is free to either disengage from that responsibility, or to re-enlist. This system has worked well, because people do not feel they are signing their life away when they get involved. No matter how frustrating or unproductive their experience is, it will last for a limited period. And if they have a good experience, they can recommit to it after their period of commitment ends.

Timing

You may not want to get involved in the work of the church immediately. Some people feel more comfortable about involvement after they have been part of the church for a while. Even if you believe that it may take you a few months before you're ready to use your gifts for the benefit of the church, do your homework before that time comes. (Don't wait *too* long, though. Studies have shown that if a person waits more than six months, the chances of ever taking that first step and getting involved are slim.) Determine whether or not a church you are seriously considering as your church home would provide you with the types of opportunities for service that you need. You don't want to go to all the effort of finding a church, making yourself at home, then realizing that you will be frustrated in your attempts to serve.

9

Direction and Leadership

I'm a pro basketball fanatic. I love to follow the progress of different teams, and analyze their chances of going all the way to the championships.

As I study the performance of the various teams, I am constantly impressed with the importance of leadership. It seems like every year there are one or two teams loaded with talented players, but saddled with an inept coach. Those teams play in a disorganized way, the players take on bad attitudes, and losing eventually becomes a way of life. After the coach is released and a new coach hired, often those teams rebound and begin playing up to their potential. Why? Because they are led by a person with vision and good leadership skills.

The Bible provides similar admonitions. When Paul wrote his first letter to the church in Corinth, he was perturbed because that church was plagued by poor leadership. All manner of corruption was allowed to transpire, causing Paul to write a lengthy and fiery letter of reproach. In the Books of Samuel, we read about how the Israelites suffered a time of difficulty because they had insisted on being like the other nations, and having a king. They chose Saul, who got the nation into many a bad situation, before he was replaced by a superior leader, David.

In the complex world in which we live, leadership is as important as ever. An organization without strong leadership, whether it is a business, a church, or a sports team, is an organization destined to failure. Without a clear sense of direction, a firm concept of how to accomplish that direction, and a motivated group of people interested in following the game plan, there is little hope that any church will have a successful ministry.

In the past, I have studied what makes churches grow. Perhaps the most critical factors that lead to growth are vision and leadership. It is virtually impossible to find a church that has experienced significant growth despite the absence of effective leaders who possessed a clear vision of what the church could be, and how it could achieve that status.

Vision is the ability to understand the history, the present condition, and the potential of the church, and to conceive a plan for action that will maximize the ministry potential. More often than not, vision is a result of having spent much time absorbing the facts about the community, knowing the resources upon which the church can call (people, funding, facilities, equipment, etc.), and devising sound but creative strategies for moving forward. Vision always entails progress: it is never satisfied with the status quo.

Leadership is the ability to put the plans into practice, and to accomplish the specified objectives through the skillful management of people, time, and tangible resources. A good leader is one who is able to motivate people; one who is capable of making good decisions, even under pressure or in conditions of uncertainty; one who can guide people through actions as well as words.

Unfortunately, my research also showed that thousands of churches in this country lack at least one of these vital qualities. Why should that matter to you as you are searching for a church? Because people do not like being associated with a church in which there is no sense of purpose, no real direction for the future, no plans on how to accomplish meaningful ministry outcomes, and no individual to stimulate interest and enthusiasm in the people whose efforts will determine whether or not the church is effective.

In short, nobody likes to be a loser. And while attending a church without vision or without leadership does not make you a loser, neither does it help you to be the kind of effective servant that God intends for you to be. While it is possible for one strong and capable individual to come into a church and help turn it around by force of vision, that scenario is the exception to the rule. More often, what happens is that an individual attends a church that has no leadership or no vision, and gets dragged down with the rest of the congregation.

How do you detect whether a church has adequate direction and leadership?

Direction

One of my favorite passages in the Bible is Luke 14:28-30, in which Jesus chides his followers for failing to plan. He asks who would be foolish enough to start constructing a building without first figuring out if they have enough resources to complete the structure. No matter how badly the building is needed, or how wonderful a site is available on which to place the building, if construction stops midway through the process because the owner cannot afford to pay the remaining cost of the labor and materials, then he is actually worse off than before he started. Now, not only is he without his money, but he's stuck with a half-finished building that is of no value to anyone!

A church without a detailed plan for ministry is in the same quandary as the foolish builder. The chances of a church stumbling into a successful ministry are not good. Indeed, a study of the churches that are making a real impact on the world shows that they have carefully examined the conditions, intensely studied the options that they have for activity, and developed a plan for action based upon their deliberations. This is the same process followed by all of the highly profitable companies that are leaders in their fields of business.

As you investigate churches, try to find out if those congregations in which you have a real interest have taken the time and trouble to develop meaningful plans for the future of the ministry. In some churches, the plans may be formal, written documents that are based upon months of studies, discussions, congregational meetings, and the like. In other churches, especially smaller congregations, the plans may simply be a verbal agreement among the pastor and several key lay leaders about the goals and directions of the church. Regardless of what form the plans take, try to find out what they entail. The nature of those plans will reveal much about the character of the church, and whether it is the type of group with which you wish to be associated.

Churches typically have one of two orientations in their planning. Some churches are very inward-looking. This means that the church is primarily concerned about taking care of the felt needs of its own members. There is relatively little concern about reaching out to others with the gospel or with related services. Their philosophy is that the church must take care of the people that God has led to the church, and help those individuals to be healthy and whole Christians so that each one can be freed to engage in a personal ministry.

The alternative is for the church to be outward-looking. These churches focus on getting the good news of the gospel—namely, that people can be saved by accepting Jesus Christ as their Savior—to as many people as possible. The church, in this perspective, is simply a facilitator of evangelism, preparing members to spread the Word, and providing them with a place where they can come for encouragement, and where they can bring nonbelievers who are seeking answers.

Some churches have managed to achieve a balance between these two strategies. Such a congregation is equally interested in leading people to Christ as in servicing the needs of those who have already been brought to salvation. Achieving such a balance is neither easy nor common. It takes special leadership and a dedicated membership who are constantly searching the Scriptures for guidance.

Your task, of course, is to determine which type of church you would most like to be a part of at this stage of your spiritual development. I have known a number of people who began their Christian life in a church at one end of the inward/outward continuum, and after a few years desired a change in focus. Once again, you need to be honest with yourself, and discover what your true needs are—an emphasis on the inward or on the outward orientation.

As you evaluate the plans and goals of a church, also be sure to determine whether or not the church is really in touch with what is happening in society. Jesus told his followers that they were to be in the world, but not of it. (John 17:14-16; James 4:4; 1 John 2:15-17) In other words, although we live in America and are called to minister to the people around us, we should not tacitly accept the values of the surrounding community in order to do so.

To minister effectively, we need to *understand* the values and problems of other people so that we can realistically address their needs and their questions about our faith. But God has called us to live according to *his* standards and values, no matter how different or foolish that may seem to others. As you examine a church, ask whether or not it recognizes the difference between God's values and those of the community. Explore how sensitive the body is to the issues and problems that are confronting people within the community—whether they be alcoholism, pornography, divorce, drug abuse, loneliness, or any of the dozens of other concerns or ungodly perspectives that exist throughout America. How is the church seeking to address those needs in its ministry?

Using the Bible as our standard for evaluation, I believe that there are four qualities, related to vision, which a church should possess in order to have a dynamic and healthy ministry, both to those within the church, and those on the outside. A church with vision will:

1. seek to unite its members in Christian love and understanding; as the family of Christ, we can only make a substantial impact on the world if our faith impacts the way we live, and impresses others that Jesus Christ does, in fact, make us better and more whole people;

2. develop ways of furthering people's knowledge of Jesus Christ and the Word of God, toward solidifying

their security in their faith, and their ability both to defend and to share their faith;

3. communicate freely, expressing opposing viewpoints without causing personal divisions or animosities; the consideration of new ideas is critical to both the intellectual and emotional strengthening of the body;

4. equip people to do a meaningful ministry, one which they have been called by God to perform.

When you visit a church, listen to the sermon. Examine the content in the handouts you receive. Observe the graphics used in the flyers and others publications of the church. Does it seem that the church understands what is happening in the world today? Is it addressing real problems, the tough stuff that we have to contend with day after day, or is it pontificating with easy but unrealistic and impractical solutions? Does it convey a sense of vision, as described above, toward having a ministry that will help to change lives for the better?

If you are going to grow as a Christian, you need a church that will keep you in touch with reality, and prepare you to deal with the complexities and hardships of life.

Leadership

What kind of leaders does the church have?

Effective, growing churches have leaders—both the paid staff and the lay leaders—who possess several qualities, including the following:

• they *know the content of the Bible* and are consistently attempting to use that knowledge in how they teach, preach, counsel, and recommend directions for the church to pursue;

• they have *authority* within the church, but they do not abuse that privilege. They are open to new ideas, and are not threatened by new information or fresh perspectives from other people;

• they perceive their role, as leaders, to be *enabling* the church to realize its fullest potential, as accomplished through the efforts of each and every member of the congregation;

• they *care about people;*

• they are constantly striving to *improve their relationship with God* through prayer, Bible study, and leading a holy life.

As you study a church, what clues do you receive about the nature of the leaders? Are they more concerned about their own position and power within the church, or about the ability of the people in the church to serve God and grow spiritually? Do they look upon their leadership responsibilities as "just a job," or as a privilege through which they can serve God? Are they the type of men and women whom you would like to work for, even if your work for them is only on a volunteer basis?

Realize that the answers to these questions may not be readily apparent after one or two visits. To truly know the leaders of the church, and to determine how well you would fit into the congregation may take more time and might require the development of deeper relationships.

Also be sensitive to the activity that happens at the church. Is it orderly, or does chaos seem to prevail? While you do not want to make hasty judgments, one sign of a well-conceived and well-directed church is an orderly flow of people and events.

Churches have a significantly better chance of

growing and meeting people's needs if they do *not* revolve around the pastor. The pastor holds a position of great responsibility, and is usually a central figure in the leadership and the decision-making of the church. However, God called for churches to be bodies of people in which everyone is involved, and everyone shares the responsibilities. It is the sign of a mature and healthy church to have a leadership structure in which the pastor is but one of many individuals who have a major stake.

The role of the pastor, beyond teaching and counseling the congregation, is to act as a team captain, working alongside of the people, doing those things which are necessary to make the church grow, and grow together as a family.

Consider the Future

Vision and leadership are important in the church, not just because of the way it impacts your current level of fulfillment from the church, but because of the role they play in your own spiritual future.

As you become a committed part of a church, using the gifts bestowed upon you by God, you will undoubtedly want to be part of a team ministry; you will want to have a sense of forging new trails in the community and reaping success in your ministry efforts.

To the best of your ability, evaluate the leadership of the church, and try to see your own relationship as a member to that leadership team and strategy. Is it a good fit?

10
Which Is Better—
Large or Small?

The size of the entities with which we are involved is often a key consideration in our decision-making. Take the size of the community in which you live. You could probably have chosen between a small, remote town, a suburban community, and a large city. Whether consciously or not, you made your selection on the basis of how well the community you selected fit your personality and your lifestyle needs at the time you made the choice. Similarly, you may have had an opportunity to choose between seeking a job at a large corporation, a mid-sized company, or a small firm. Again, while size was not the only criterion you considered, chances are good that the size of the company played an important role in your choice.

When it comes to selecting a church, the size of the congregation may well be a key factor. Churches take on different personalities as their size changes, and the size of a church helps to shape the nature of its ministry.

It is interesting that of the more than three hundred thousand Protestant churches in our country, the vast

114/How to Find *Your* Church

majority of them have fewer than one hundred active members. Yet, the churches that we typically hear about in the media and through other sources are those which have a thousand or more participants. Statistics indicate that the fastest-growing churches usually end up with somewhere between three thousand and ten thousand members, accumulated within a period of explosive growth that took just five years or less. It is odd that, in a society in which people are demanding greater personalization, and in which bigger is no longer assumed to be better, the number of members in the average church is climbing each year, and the number of "megachurches" also continues to escalate.

Certainly, large churches have advantages, but small congregations have their own unique and appealing qualities as well. What are some of the trade-offs to ponder if you encounter attractive churches of different-sized congregations?

Large Churches

If you have ever visited a large church—say, a congregation that includes more than a thousand active members—you probably come away with a mixture of emotions. The first two churches to which I belonged after graduating from college were small—twenty-five and ninety members, respectively. Upon moving west, we wound up in a megachurch—more than three thousand active members. Talk about culture shock! After my first visit, I didn't know what to make of the place. And, yet, it was a positive enough experience that I came back again. And again. But it did take me some time to adjust, and to sort out what I was experiencing and feeling about such a comparatively monstrous "family."

My own experiences with large churches, and the input I've received from others involved with such congregations, indicates that they possess a number of magnetic qualities.

Many people feel comfortable in such churches because the size affords them an anonymity which cannot be achieved in a small church. Although most church leaders shudder at the thought of promoting a blend-in-with-the-woodwork mentality within the church, anonymity is not always bad. There are stages in people's lives when they wish to go along for the ride, rather than be in the spotlight. For some individuals, when they join their first church, or when they have recently made a commitment to Christ and are not clear as to what that commitment means, the easy-going nature of the large church might be more attractive and productive. Sometimes you can grow a lot more as an observer than as a focal point—especially if you are in an exploratory stage of your own development. In large congregations, there are ways of attaining your fair share of the spotlight, but you generally initiate the decision to do so; you are less likely to be actively pursued for service than you would be in a small church.

As the Bible teaches, there is a season for everything—and that probably includes involvement in the workings of the church. Rushing into service may leave you with a bad taste in your mouth, if you are not ready to engage in such service. Some of my friends have found that the anonymity factor of a large congregation made integration into the flow of the church less threatening for them.

The large numbers also means that there is greater opportunity to interact with other people. Depending upon the nature of the congregation, you may or may not find that there are many people with whom you desire to build closer relationships. Nevertheless, the mathematical possibilities are greater at large churches.

One of the great distinctions of large churches is that they generally provide a wider range of programs, choices, and opportunities for all people. A small congregation does not have the resources—or, perhaps, the breadth of needs—to justify and support a full menu of Sunday-school classes, social events, teaching programs, and other events that are targeted to very narrowly defined niches. A large congregation can do so without overexertion. This enhancement of the variety offered can prove to be especially beneficial to people who are in times of transition in their lives—whether it be spiritual, emotional, or psychological. The breadth of options makes it easier for a person to explore different avenues toward optimizing personal growth.

While it could be argued either way, some people contend that large churches are more likely to be characterized by services and programs of superior quality than is typically found in small churches. If this is the case, it is a chicken-egg proposition: Which came first, many members because of superior quality, or superior quality because of many members? It doesn't matter, really. The point is that many people have found that a large church offers a level of ministry unmatched by the smaller churches which they attended, whether that was caused by the larger budgets, the greater programmatic variety, or other factors associated with large churches.

And while it is not an ironclad rule, large churches might be expected to have superior facilities to that of a small church. Only those congregations with hundreds of members would have a need for (and the capacity to maintain) gymnasiums, auditoriums, vans, sophisticated electronic equipment, active lending libraries, tape ministries, and so forth.

In addition, many large churches work hard at offering a small-church experience within the structure and reality of the larger congregation. They attempt to provide the best of both worlds: the benefits of a large church (i.e., quality of staff, services, programs, and facilities) while providing the personalized touch that characterizes small churches. The personal touch is achieved by breaking the church into smaller functional units: small group Bible studies, specialized choirs, Sunday-school classes based on narrow age groups, etc.

Small Churches

Congregations of two hundred or fewer people are a different breed of organization than the megachurch—not necessarily inferior, just different. To many people they are a more appropriate church with which to be affiliated.

One compelling reason is the chance to get to know all of the people in the church. If a church is truly a family, then the smaller the body the easier it is to have a relationship with each person.

For some people, the smallness of the church is important because it enables them to have more interaction with the church leaders, and to learn from their experience and wisdom. And there is the sense of having easier accessibility to the decision-makers within the church, whether they be the paid staff or the lay leaders. Lines of communication tend to be more direct.

By the same token, the leaner hierarchy also imputes a greater degree of responsibility to each of the people involved with the small church. On the one hand, this means greater opportunities for service, and for assuming a leadership post within the church. An individual can find that he or she gains considerable influence within a small church in a relatively short period of time.

On the other hand, small churches maintain higher expectations of performance for their members, since they are so heavily dependent upon the labor of each member. And for those who do become involved in the work of the church, along with the acquired influence and authority come the burdens of responsibility and accountability. What you do in a small church may be more visible, and may have a greater ultimate impact on the health of the church than a similar position in a large church.

Organizationally, small churches tend to have a simpler structure. If you are seeking a family-like experience in which simplicity is of value, the small congregation may be better suited to your needs.

In short, it is much easier to achieve a sense of "ownership" of the church in a small congregation. Knowing the people, being a part of the decision-making body, being held more accountable for your actions—all of these conditions promote a heightened sense of the church truly being a part of your family and personality.

Choosing One or the Other

There is always the temptation to suggest that one type of church or the other is superior, and should be given more serious consideration. However, if my experience is any indication, as we mature as individuals and as Christians, we move through different stages of development during which churches of different sizes may best fit our particular needs.

In my case, when I first accepted Christ, Christianity was a new ball game for me to learn. Being involved in tiny congregations was a blessing because I was able to receive the kind of personalized attention from the leaders that never could have been received had I been a new member at a megachurch. The simplicity of the church structures enabled me to concentrate on specific aspects of my faith without paying much attention to organization.

As I matured in my faith, and at the same time moved on to megachurches, those experiences introduced me to many new ministry opportunities. And by that time I was ready to explore some of those options in a more realistic and committed fashion.

Overall, then, I see my own movement through a maze of various-sized congregations as God's providentially bringing me to churches that have offered just the right combination of opportunities, nurturing, and challenges for my successive stages of spiritual development. No church I have ever joined was better or worse than any of the others. Each was right for my needs at the time. And the size of the congregation, and the related benefits and limitations created by the size, was an integral component of my experience.

11
Church Location and Facilities

As one who makes his living by doing marketing research, I am frequently asked to discuss trends in attitudes and lifestyle. Among the trends that characterize American adults today, and the baby-boom generation in particular, are the desire for convenience, the expectation of excellence, and the need for options in decision-making.

These trends have helped me to understand why we live in a nation with more than three hundred thousand Christian churches—and still continue to create new ones, even though the lion's share of the old ones haven't been filled to reach their capacity and their potential. At first, this seemed to me to be outright foolishness, a wasteful allocation of resources.

Yet, new churches are continually being planted because there are perceived needs that are not being satisfied by the existing churches. And those needs are frequently related to the three trends identified above.

For instance, in your community there may not be a church of the type you are seeking (e.g., small congregation, charismatic, non-denominational, majority of attenders under forty years of age). Thus, the church options are not adequate to meet your needs, and a new church that comes along and satisfies those requirements will appeal to you.

Perhaps there is such a church, but it is located three communities away, requiring a time-consuming commute and precluding the opportunity to meet people who live in your area. Or, maybe, the church in which you are most interested has only a single Sunday-morning service that meets at 8:30 in the morning—far too early to prepare your family, get out the door and into the sanctuary on-time. The problem is one of convenience.

Location

There is a significant difference between the concern of church leaders and church visitors related to church location. The leaders frequently worry about "sight accessibility": Does the church building's location offer enough visibility to attract newcomers? Many churches agonize over the fact that they are located on a side street or in some remote location, difficult for visitors to find.

Visitors, on the other hand, do not have that concern, since they *found* the church and are inside its doors! They are more concerned about how long it takes to get to that location from their home, and what kind of hassles (e.g., traffic, unsuitable roads, distance from the home) they have to contend with in order to get there.

Church growth specialists inform us that people generally will not travel more than six miles to get to a church. This may not seem like a long distance; perhaps you would have expected most people seeking a good church to be willing to drive farther than that.

Actually, many people start out on their church-selection quest quite willing to travel three times as many miles if it brings them to the spiritual home they've had in mind. Unfortunately, many people who wind up choosing a church fifteen or twenty miles from home find out that one of two things happens: Some learn (the hard way) that the commute is so long that it discourages them from coming back for other church activities; they unintentionally become "Sunday-morning members." Other people, not content to limit their church involvement to Sunday mornings, decide that maybe the church wasn't the ideal choice after all, and re-initiate their church search. This time, they specifically look for a congregation that is within a short drive from their home.

I can relate to this quandary. While living in Chicago, my wife and I found the church of our dreams—but it was twenty-five miles away. We faithfully drove back and forth several times a week for quite a while: Sunday-morning worship services, Wednesday-evening services, and other evenings for special programs (youth night) and meetings (committees, special speakers, or social events). At the end of one year, when we were working on our tax returns, we noticed that we had driven more miles to and from church than we had driven to our jobs. The time and cost of doing so was a considerable commitment.

Traffic problems can make matters worse, although, upon returning to Los Angeles, we realized that traffic would not be a problem for us. L.A. is known for its bumper-to-bumper freeways; but we quickly found out that there is more traffic on the freeways and surface streets at 3 a.m. on a Tuesday morning than on Sunday mornings between 8 and 11. Indeed, most of the other cars on the road during that time are other people driving to a destination at which they can worship their God—either to a church, or to the local car wash!

How far are you willing to travel to get to a good church? Consider how many round-trips to the church you would likely make during a typical week, and how much time you need to dedicate solely to travel. This reality may reduce, if not eliminate, the appeal of certain churches.

One other element related to location is the type of neighborhood within which a church is located. Imagine yourself (and your children, if you have any) on the streets around the church late at night. Is it the type of area in which you feel safe and comfortable? If it is an area in which personal safety is a legitimate concern, does the church have a means of looking after its people when they are at church? Some very dynamic churches are located in the heart of high-crime areas, and are helping to restore those neighborhoods to health and safety. But they have also established systems for guarding the welfare of their people. Location and personal security can make a big difference in the anxiety level with which you come to worship and interact.

Facilities

Frequently, people visit a church and leave perplexed: They finally found a church that had all the items on their wish list, but they still have a nagging doubt about whether or not the church is right for them. More often than not, the lingering doubt was caused by the subconscious realization that the church's facilities did not pass muster.

Examine the facilities and equipment of the church you are visiting. Does it possess the kind of rooms and equipment that will enable it to address the needs and expectations you have? If the church does not have those items, you may have good reason to wonder how effective the church is likely to be in expanding to meet new needs, or enlarging the scope of existing programs to accommodate new growth within the church.

The facilities of a church tell you a lot about their priorities, and even their self-esteem. Churches which have rundown, dilapidated facilities—peeling paint, broken windows, ripped carpets, a broken sound system, a leaking roof, huge potholes in the parking lot— probably lack enough self-confidence in, and love for the church to house a vibrant ministry. While you may catch a church or two in the midst of a capital improvements campaign, and ought not to judge too hastily, be sensitive to the condition of the facilities. You may even determine that if, despite a healthy size and reasonable budget, the facilities have been allowed to deteriorate, it is evidence of either poor financial management, or a flagrant disinterest in maintaining the buildings and grounds.

What types of facilities do they have? Parking may be a primary consideration. There are few things more maddening to me than to have to park several blocks from a church and have to walk five to ten minutes to get there—especially if the windchill factor is below zero, or it's raining cats and dogs! I've been to other churches which have unpaved parking lots—no problem until spring arrives and turns that lot into a swamp.

The size of the worship hall can be important. Perhaps it is overcrowded, or way too large for the size of the congregation. If this mismatch between space and number of people has little chance of being rectified, it may inhibit your ability to have a meaningful experience.

In many cases, the very size of the worship hall imparts valuable clues about the potential of the church. If the hall is jammed, and there are no plans for expansion, the church cannot hope to grow. If the hall is empty, and there are few visitors or new members coming forth, at some point the congregation may be faced with hardships related to the care and maintenance of the building. Both of these situations have their own ramifications—financially, socially, and related to the potential for your own spiritual growth.

What about other facilities, such as classrooms for Sunday school or other events, or a gymnasium for youth or social activities? Not every church needs a gym, or a building filled with classrooms: again, the personality and goals of the church determine the needs. But does the church, given its facilities, satisfy *your* needs?

Equipment is another matter to consider, although when placed in the overall picture, it may be but a minor consideration. Even so, many people I've spoken with have expressed their irritation over the lack of simple pieces of equipment, such as a VCR or a slide projector. The absence of such equipment can sometimes hinder attempts to reach out to people in ways that are creative, entertaining, and effective. The abject refusal of a church to purchase such equipment, especially if the obstacle is based upon principle rather than finances, also provides you with an insight into the mindset of the leadership.

Along with equipment, you may wish to consider the educational resources of the church, especially if you have children who would be enrolled in a Sunday school or other youth program. Take account of the curriculum resources on hand, and the supplemental resources available. This could prove to be a crucial bit of information as you make your final selection.

Keep Your Perspective

When you narrow down your selections to the final few, it would be unfortunate to eliminate an otherwise spiritually mature and alive church solely on the basis of inadequate facilities or location. Truly, God did not call us to worship him only if the pews were comfortable and the streets outside the church had sufficient lighting. However, we need to recognize our own personalities and idiosyncrasies, too. Perhaps attending a church that does not have the most modern or the most dazzling facilities and equipment would be difficult—but perhaps it's also an opportunity for us to grow personally, by focusing on the central elements of the church experience, and working to enhance the deficiencies existing within the church.

12
Special Programs

"I didn't just want a church where the services were good, but that's all they had to offer. Christianity was a whole new world to me, and I wanted to soak up as much of it as I could. The church seemed to me to be the place where I ought to be able to turn to get the kind of guidance and help that I needed. Besides, I had no idea where else to turn for the type of religious education that I was looking for."

That's how one woman we interviewed described her search for a church. As a new Christian, she recognized that there was so much for her to learn and experience—simply attending a one-hour worship service once a week could not satisfy her hunger to know God in a more intimate way. To her credit, she did not settle for the first few churches she visited, which offered little beyond the Sunday-morning service. Committed to finding a church that had programs that would meet her needs, she eventually visited a church that was just what she was seeking: one which offered a range of programs and ministry opportunities, spread

130/How to Find *Your* Church

throughout the week, open to anyone interested.

Earlier, in chapter 8, we discussed the virtues of finding a church that will provide you with opportunities to serve others. But what about being served *by* others in the church? One of the crucial responsibilities of a church is to lead its members to personal growth in all areas of their lives. You cannot adequately minister to others until you have first been ministered to. If, for instance, you wish to teach the Bible to children, it is imperative that you understand the Bible first. You might need to spend time learning through a Sunday-school class, or a small-group study, or a Bible-training course before you engage in such teaching. Or, if you wish to lead other people to Christ, you must first be confident in your own faith, and have a solid enough grasp of the basics of your faith that you will be able to articulate it in a logical, defensible, and understandable manner. Once again, this may require that you spend some time absorbing information and experiences through various programs or activities offered by your church, before you can effectively engage in reaching out to others.

While you certainly want to avoid the danger of looking at a church only as a place from which you can receive benefits, it is important to find a church family where you will be able to derive spiritual strength and nourishment. In many cases you may find that, even in the context of gaining benefits from various church programs, you will also have opportunities to participate in those programs in leadership roles.

Common Types of Programs

Most churches have some type of educational

programs related to the Bible. The most popular format is Sunday-school classes which meet every Sunday, either before or after the worship service. Often (especially in larger churches), there will be several classes from which you can choose. Those classes may be based upon age groups, marital status, occupational interests, issues and discussion topics, or other concepts.

Whenever possible, my wife and I have found it to be fruitful to visit several different classes before settling upon one. We have also found that, to get the most out of the classes, we are better off if we make a commitment to that group, enabling us to get to know the people, to find opportunities for service, and to glean the most from the teaching. Often, the Sunday-school class becomes like a church within the church, providing many of the benefits you are seeking from a church, within that smaller context.

Additional options may include small groups that meet regularly to study and discuss the Bible, at a place other than the church itself. Churches call these groups by various names: Bible study groups, fellowship groups, home groups, and so forth. The group might convene for the purpose of studying the Bible, praying, or simply getting to know and encouraging each other. (Most small groups actually meet with the intention of satisfying two or three of those purposes.) The groups generally meet once a week, and each meeting lasts between one and two hours. Research has shown that the small group programs of churches are among the most important means of enabling people to feel like they really belong to the church, and to establish meaningful personal ties with other church members.

Another option is some type of "discipleship" program, in which one of the church leaders takes a handful of people under his or her wing, to strengthen them in their faith and prepare them for positions of greater leadership responsibility.

Many churches also provide other kinds of educational opportunities. Training sessions and seminars are occasionally sponsored, addressing topics such as how to study the Bible, how to share your faith with a nonbeliever, and steps toward discovering your spiritual gifts. Other programs may be less spiritually-oriented: voice training (perhaps as a prelude to joining the choir), English as a second language, or even light aerobics or physical fitness sessions.

Larger churches sometimes sponsor adult education classes, similar to those that might be offered in the evening at local public schools (although usually the church-sponsored classes carry no accreditation). On occasion, a church will even offer a Bible-training institute, in which pastors or Christian-college professors are drawn together to offer theological training in a seminary-like environment.

Non-educational Programs

Churches are not all serious stuff, though. Some churches have sponsored concert series, film series, and community walking tours as ways of bringing people together in a fun, relaxed atmosphere.

In fact, in some parts of the country, one of the hottest draws for a church is its sports teams, which usually compete against teams from other churches. The sports most commonly represented in such leagues are football, basketball, and softball. Some churches also feature challenge tournaments, either an intra-church tournament or a one-day competition against teams from other churches, in individual sports like tennis, racquetball, and bowling. Some of the larger churches even have their own intramural basketball, softball, or volleyball leagues.

Women often have opportunities to get involved in special church programs. The activities undertaken by such groups vary greatly, from focusing upon crafts to taking day trips to interesting historical or cultural centers, inviting inspirational speakers to address the group, or having a regular time of Bible study and prayer.

Counseling is available from some churches, for those individuals who wish to have guidance in relation to marital problems or other situations which the pastor or church staff person is qualified to handle.

The youth program at the church is generally one of the most important ancillary services provided. Beyond the Sunday-school program, it is not uncommon for a church to provide special youth programs such as social events, summer camps, mid-week youth meetings which encompass games and social activities as well as spiritual training, and some type of community service program. It seems that one way to distinguish a church that is truly alive and progressing from one that is not is by evaluating the life of the youth program. It is uncommon to find an exciting and popular youth program connected to a church that is dormant or in decline.

During the summer, you may have noticedthat many churches have what they call a "Vacation Bible School" (VBS). VBS can provide you with a chance to enroll your children during their summer vacation for one week or longer in a program that will give them special spiritual training, along with other fun activities. (Such programs also provide mothers with a break from their energetic kids for at least a few hours during the week!)

In some congregations, groups of members band together to form "prayer chains." These are people who have made a commitment to be on call for those who have special prayer needs. (It is referred to as a "chain" because the request for prayer is communicated by each member of the group calling another member.) They agree to stop whatever they are doing and pray, whenever they are called with a specific request. The existence of a prayer chain within a church suggests that the church is serious about the power and exercise of prayer as a means of communicating with God.

You may also want to explore what types of special resources are available to members. Is there a church library, with books, records, and tapes of interest to you? Are there tutors on call to assist you with some subject which you are studying? Is there a "talent bank," which you may consult if you need professional services or manual labor?

Discerning Consumerism

As you learn about the special programs that a church has to offer, keep in mind two parameters:

First, some churches seem to go for "tonnage"— that is, they offer dozens and dozens of special programs, a veritable menu of special activities. However, if none of those programs are ones in which you or your family are interested, the church might as well offer none of them, at least as far as your own needs are concerned. The church is not wrong to offer what it does, nor is it a failure because it has not provided programs in which you are interested. The church may simply be on a different wavelength than you. As you are evaluating churches, though, do not be swayed by the fact that it offers a laundry list of programs. Take a moment to consider what is being offered, and if it is relevant to your needs.

Second, as in any walk of life, there is more to evaluating a program than its mere existence, even if the program would address a keen personal interest. Try to get a sense of the *quality* of the programs provided. I have attended churches which promoted programs that sounded great. I signed up for the programs, brimming with enthusiasm and anticipation—and boy, was I disappointed! There is nothing so aggravating as leaving a session feeling that you have been ripped off—whether the squandered resource was your money, your time, or your excitement.

Also remember to keep special programs in perspective. While they may be critical to your ultimate enjoyment of the church, and to your personal growth as a Christian, the programs are but one of a number of elements of the church's life that deserve your consideration.

13
Making *Your* Choice

"It was a fascinating experience for me."

"I learned a lot about churches, and a lot about my faith, by visiting all those churches."

"It took much longer than I ever dreamed it would. But, in the end, it was worth the time and energy."

These are a few of the reactions people gave about their church exploration adventure. The majority of the people said that the experience was fruitful, providing them with a much larger understanding of their faith and how the church which they eventually chose fit within the overall framework of the Christian church in America.

But there is one key: After doing all of your homework, you do have to make a choice. After you have gone to the effort of visiting churches, observing what happens, joining in the worship and teaching times, taking notes, talking over your concerns with other people, praying about your perceptions and your selection, it's time to pick one church as your church home.

For a long time, during my second church-shopping adventure, I agonized over the final decision. Certainly, the selection was a major decision in my life, one that would impact my spiritual growth, as well as my social relationships and other meaningful aspects of my life. The last thing I wanted to do was choose the wrong church.

It finally dawned on me that, if I had done my homework properly, I couldn't make the wrong choice. Sure, I might select one church from a small group of finalists and determine after a few months of committed attendance and involvement that the church was not the right one, after all. But I would not be a loser in that case: I simply would have extended my search adventure to a longer time frame, and would have collected a greater quantity and depth of information upon which to determine the church was not the right choice. At that point, I could review my notes of other churches that were in the running, and take my next-best option.

Visitation Period

How many churches should you visit before you draw your conclusion? It depends on what you are looking for, the range of church options available to you, and your temperament. The most anyone can reasonably recommend to you is that you not settle on the first church you visit, even if it seems to be the ideal congregation for you. You should commit yourself to visiting a minimum number of churches—probably at least four—before you even begin the process.

Even if you wind up going back to the first church you visited and selecting it as your best option, do not feel that you have wasted time and effort. The insights and experiences gained from exposure to different styles of worship, different approaches to ministry, and different Christians who are also seeking to serve God, cannot be obtained any other way. And, if you're like me, as you mature in your Christianity and begin to assume positions of leadership within your church, some of the things you experienced during your visitation period will give you ideas that can be adopted or adapted by your church. Also consider that, after conducting a thorough search, you will probably feel much more confident about your final choice than if you had simply opted for the first church you encountered.

Our research found that the average church shopper will visit a particular church about four times before deciding to become part of that congregation—that is four visits, in addition to one or two visits to each of the other churches the person was evaluating.

Your Criteria

The key to your selection is knowing your needs and interests, and gaining enough relevant information about each church to make an informed decision about how well it would facilitate your growth. It is important to have a sense of what is significant to you, and what trade-offs or compromises you would be willing to make toward finding the optimal church. The appendix of this book contains the sample forms which you may wish to use or adapt for your search. Or, you may simply wish to base your decision upon your recall of each church and an instinctive determination. The former approach is more intellect-based, the latter is more emotion-driven. You must decide which approach is most appropriate for you.

Do not pressure yourself about this decision. Yes,

it is a very important choice you are making. Yes, it is a complex decision, requiring you to weigh the impact of many different factors observed under imperfect conditions. Nevertheless, remember that your choice is not necessarily final. Should you select a church that you believe will suit you but find after a reasonable trial period that things are not working out as planned, you can always change. Rather than consider yourself a poor judge of churches, or a failure for having made a less-than-optimal choice, simply consider your experience another step in the learning process. There is no penalty exacted by God upon those people who, in their earnest desire to follow his leading and worship and serve him, choose to change from one body of believers to another.

Choices and Commitments

Having said that, though, let me restate that there are advantages to sticking with a church once you have chosen it and the initial experiences are positive. It is wrong to flit from church to church every time something goes contrary to your own personal whims or desires. The church is our spiritual family, and just as divorce is not to be held as a trump card in our marital relations, neither is dumping one church for another an act that we should take lightly, or do with any regularity.

As you commit yourself to a church, you'll find that there are many advantages to sticking with that church for the long haul. By accepting the congregation as your church home, you'll have an easier time making deep and lasting friendships. You'll have a greater range and number of opportunities to be involved in activities and decision-making at the church. Longevity within the church may enhance your own feeling of roots and stability, and help to reduce your anxiety level. Perhaps more importantly, you will also be setting an example of commitment for new Christians and for youth.

One of the amazing traits about life in America is the huge number of choices we have in almost every aspect of our daily lives. Whether it is the brands of foods we choose at the supermarket, the different types of gasoline we pour into our cars, the type of medical insurance we obtain, or the church we choose to join, the number and range of options is unprecedented. In fact, if we read the way in which people in the Bible chose their church group, we learn very quickly that there was little choice. They belonged to the one Christian church that was in their community.

What difference does this make? Simply that while we can be thankful that we have options from which to choose, our focus must remain on God and how we can best worship and serve him. We must be careful not to get so picky that we abuse the options we have, and begin to taint our perspective of what a church is to be about. The primary role of the church is to bring us closer to God, through relationships, teaching, and service to others. We, too, have a responsibility to God, to our fellow Christians, and to ourselves not to become so demanding that no church will ever truly satisfy our desires.

Realize, too, that so many other people who were in your shoes have learned that the best way to fit into a church is to get involved as soon as possible. Make friends. Commit your time and talents. Take the teaching seriously. The grass may look greener on the other side, but it rarely is.

142/How to Find *Your* Church

Rest assured that God has prepared a church for you. During your search, do not forget to include him in your search. Pray for guidance and wisdom. And be sensitive to the clues which he opens up to you. He really *does* care which church you select, as it will be one of the avenues through which you are able to serve him and build your relationship with him. Count on him as your most treasured resource in your search for the right church.

Appendix

You've probably heard the expression, "You can't tell the players without a scorecard." If you visit a half dozen or more churches, you may wish that you had some type of scorecard to help you remember which churches you have visited, and what they were like. As time passes, so do the details of our experiences. Having a written record of what transpired can be a very useful tool when it comes time to make your final decision on what church to select as your church home.

There are different ways of keeping track of your experience. Some of the people we surveyed simply made a few notes on a pad, for later reference. Others took a more formal approach, and kept what amounted to a diary of their church visits. In each diary entry, they described what they experienced, how they felt about the church, and whether or not the church was worth considering as a "finalist" in the selection process.

Earlier in this book, I mentioned that you might wish to have a more detailed record of what the churches you visit have to offer. I have prepared a form that you might wish to use to track those details. Feel free to adapt it to your own special needs and interests. The form is only meant to be a sample of how you might catalog your experiences.

As a marketing researcher, I tend to be very quantitative in nature, and would even apply weights to each of the entries, to derive a weighted average of how well each church measured up. For most people, that's overkill. However, I do suggest that you organize the elements listed on the form in some arrangement that takes into account the relative importance to you of each item.

For instance, if you visit a church where the adult Sunday-school class rates a "10" but the church lacks a strong youth program, a straight mathematical evaluation of those two factors might cause the church to be somewhat unappealing. If, however, you have no children to enroll in the youth program, then the church assumes a more attractive profile. It is for this reason that I encourage you to consider the relative importance to you of each characteristic.

This form is meant to be an aide, not the final yardstick. Use it for whatever purposes you desire, and to whatever extent makes sense given your needs.

CHURCH-VISITATION REVIEW

For each of the elements listed on the following pages, enter a number from 1 to 10 in the space provided. A "1" indicates the church you visited is totally inadequate for your needs in that area; a "10," suggests the church provides exactly what you are looking for.

When you are evaluating the relative appeal of churches, be sure to also take into account how important each of the measured characteristics is in your own decision. (If a category such as "athletic facilities" is totally unimportant to you, you may wish to simply cross it off the form.) There is no sense attending a church that is great in all the areas you don't care about, but flounders when it comes to the things you feel are most important— regardless of what the mathematics of this evaluation system indicate.

Evaluation Criteria	Church name _____ Location _____ Date of visit _____	Church name _____ Location _____ Date of visit _____	Church name _____ Location _____ Date of visit _____
A. Spiritual beliefs about:			
God			
Jesus Christ			
the Holy Spirit			
communion			
the Bible			
sin, Satan			
salvation			
sacraments			
purpose of life			
the role of women			
baptism			
spiritual gifts			
social issues			
B. Worship experience:			
sermons			
music			
service contents			
style of worship			
participation			
tone of worship			
prayer			
attitude toward worship			

C. Leadership:	1	2	3
sense of vision			
active laity			
opportunities to lead			
enough leaders			
discernible priorities			
knowledge of the Bible			
commitment to the Bible			
D. People:			
friendly			
people your age			
committed			
involved with each other			
accepting of differences			
people you know are there			
congregational unity			
E. Special programs:			
adult Sunday school			
youth program			
missions activity			
Bible study groups			
women's programs			
sports program			
community outreach			
evangelism			
prayer			
social events			
discipleship			
issues seminars			
entertainment events			
counseling			

F. Opportunity for service:	1	2	3
match members' gifts			
with needs			
multiple opportunities			
appealing opportunities			
laity ownership of programs			
express gratitude for service			
time commitments expected			
G. Structure:			
easy to meet people			
people involved			
ministers accessible			
well-organized			
method of government			
focus on people, not programs			
support groups			
in touch with community			
communications tools			
H. Size:			
membership			
youth program			
I. Location:			
security of area			
distance from home			
part of community			

J. Facilities and equipment:	1	2	3
condition of buildings			
sufficient space			
adequate parking			
athletic facilities			
classroom space			
library			
sound equipment			
video equipment			
K. Affiliations:			
denomination			
community associations			
national coalitions			
L. Follow-up by church:			
contacted			
reasons for their interest			
introductory class			

Bibliography

Backman, Milton Jr., *Christian Churches of America*. Salt Lake City: Brigham Young University Press, 1976.

Banks, Robert and Julia, *The Home Church*. Sutherland, NSW, Australia: Albatross Books, 1986.

Barna, George, *Marketing the Church*, Colorado Springs: NavPress, 1988.

_____. *America 2000: What the Trends Mean for Christianity*, Glendale, Cal.: Barna Research Group, 1989.

Callahan, Kennon L., *Twelve Keys to an Effective Church*, San Francisco: Harper & Row, 1983.

Douglas, J. D., *The New Bible Dictionary*, Wheaton, Ill.: Tyndale House Publishers, 1982.

Evans, William, *Great Doctrines of the Bible*, Chicago: Moody Press, 1979.

Gibbs, Eddie, *I Believe in Church Growth*, London: Hodder and Stoughton, 1985.

Gilbert, Larry, *Team Ministry*, Lynchburg, Virginia: Church Growth Institute, 1987.

Graham, Billy, *The Holy Spirit*, Waco, Texas: Word Books, 1978.

Hayford, Jack W., *Worship His Majesty*, Waco, Texas: Word Books, 1987.

Hesselgrave, David, *Planting Churches Cross-Culturally*, Grand Rapids, Mich.: Baker Book House, 1979.

Hocking, David, *The World's Greatest Church*, Long Beach, Cal.: Sounds of Grace Ministries, 1976.

Jacquet, Constant H. Jr., *Yearbook of American and Canadian Churches—1988*, Nashville: Abingdon Press, 1988.

Little, Paul, *Know What You Believe*, Wheaton, Ill.: Victor Books/Scripture Press, 1987.

MacArthur, John Jr., *The Anatomy of a Church*, Chicago: Moody Press, 1986.

McGavran, Donald, and George G. Hunter, *Church Growth: Strategies That Work*, Nashville: Abingdon Press, 1980.

Moberg, David O., *The Church as a Social Institution*, Grand Rapids, Mich.: Baker Book House, 1984.

Riggs, Charles, *Learning to Walk*, Minneapolis: World Wide Publications, 1987.

Rostin, Leo, *Religions in America*, New York: Simon and Schuster, 1975.

Snyder, Howard A., *Liberating the Church*, Downers Grove, Ill.: InterVarsity Press, 1983.

Strong, James, *The Strong's Exhaustive Concordance of the Bible*, Nashville: Thomas Nelson Publishers, 1985.

Towns, Elmer, John Vaughan, and David Seifert, *The Complete Book of Church Growth*, Wheaton, Ill.: Tyndale House, 1981.

Watson, David, *I Believe in the Church*, Grand Rapids, Mich.: Eerdmans Publishing, 1979.